STEAM PACKET
190

MILES COWSILL • JOHN HENDY

CONTRIBUTORS BARRY EDWARDS, RICHARD KIRKMAN AND RICHARD SEVILLE

Ferry
Publications

Stan Basnett

Published 2020
Copyright © Ferry Publications, PO Box 33, Ramsey, Isle of Man, British Isles
All rights reserved.
ISBN: 9781911268369

CONTENTS

FOREWORD

It is with great delight that I have been asked to provide the foreword for this extensively researched and well-written book, which has been published to celebrate 190 years of the Isle of Man Steam Packet Company.

As the world's oldest continually operating passenger shipping company, it is no surprise that we have a long and illustrious history, which is as fascinating as it is diverse, and it is certainly one of which we are extremely proud.

Since operations began in 1830, the company has experienced the modernisation of ferry travel, played a part in two World Wars, been involved in several changes of ownership and, of course, maintained vital sea links, connecting the Isle of Man to England and Ireland for almost 200 years. Now that the Company is owned by the Manx people, albeit on an arms-length commercial basis, I sincerely hope that we will be able to celebrate our 200th anniversary in style.

Over the course of these two centuries, a consistency which has been maintained throughout is the progressive and enterprising nature of the Steam Packet Company and this book is a fitting tribute to those past and present 'family members' who have tirelessly served the Company and the Island.

Looking back to 1830, the Company was launched at a time when there was a lot of competition on the Irish Sea, but the management and crew of the day were dedicated to securing a stable and reliable service for the people of the Isle of Man. That legacy is one we uphold to this day. Indeed, today we carry around 600,000 passengers and 170,000 vehicles each year, in addition to acting as the Island's lifeline for vital freight and commodity services.

As proud as my colleagues and I are to represent a company with such an esteemed maritime history, we are also looking

Mark Woodward

forward to the next part of our journey; continuing to play our valued role in the Manx community, serving the people of the Isle of Man.

The User Agreement, which had dictated how the Company provides services to the Island as a private company, has now been replaced by a new Sea Services Agreement negotiated with the Isle of Man Government. This will take the Company forward to the middle of this century.

This very special shipping company remains committed to the long-term future of sea services for the Island, strengthened further by its new stakeholders, Island residents, and the design and introduction of a new purpose-built vessel over the next few years. This new vessel will replace the *Ben-my-Chree* which, having already served the Island with distinction for more than 22 years, will remain available as a back-up vessel thereby giving the Island a security of service it has not seen for a long time.

In such a milestone year, Steam Packet 190 is a magnificent tribute to the company's achievements, both in words as well as a rich variety of photographs. These include a wealth of new and interesting illustrations of past vessels and individuals associated with the company.

I wish everyone who has contributed to this publication a sincere thank you. I can promise in return that, with a strong long-term platform in place to deliver continued investment and sea services for the Island, the company looks ahead to the future with optimism.

Mark Woodward
Chief Executive Officer

CHAPTER ONE

THE FOUNDATION OF THE COMPANY

In 1767 the British Government passed an Act authorising their Post Office to conduct mail to and from the Isle of Man, to establish post offices and post roads as necessary and to establish a packet boat between the port of Whitehaven (Cumberland) and Douglas.

Prior to 1767 the Isle of Man was not within the remit of the Post Office and the conveyance of mail to and from the Island was at best erratic and not secure even for official communications, although for seventeen years prior to the Act a privately-owned packet boat had operated a service between Whitehaven and Douglas.

Under the new Act, Douglas was made a sub-office of Whitehaven and the mail contract was awarded to a Whitehaven syndicate to provide a weekly return sailing, weather permitting, for a fee of £150 per annum. The sailings were very much dependent on the vagaries of the weather - in 1813 the mail packet actually completed fifty two round voyages, yet in December 1821 only one round voyage was possible in six weeks owing to persistent gales. Given fair weather the passage took about six hours and the fare was 10/6d (52.5p). Adverse weather was still to cause delays to the post and smuggling, so long a way of life around the ports of the Irish Sea, was often more profitable than the mail!

Until 1819, communication between the Isle of Man and the rest of the British Isles remained the domain of sailing vessels most of which were traders. The *Duke of Athol* and *Lapwing* however also carried mail and passengers. The port of despatch for the mail was Whitehaven which, being exposed to westerly gales, caused many delays.

Dissatisfaction with the service continued with local merchants and officials taking matters into their own hands and passing letters to masters of vessels and passengers bound for Liverpool for onward transmission on arrival. Not only was the Governor amongst those complaining but also the Bishop and the commanding officer of the garrison at Castle Rushen.

Steamer Services

The advent of steamer services on the Irish Sea and elsewhere by the second decade of the nineteenth century saw the Whitehaven contractors and the Post Office under more threat to improve their service. The Whitehaven contractors acquired a bigger sailing vessel and undertook to provide eighty sailings a year. Adverse weather and competition conspired against them so much that the islanders, to the annoyance of the Post Office, continued to use the steamers and the port of Liverpool as their preferred option.

The first mention of a steamer in Manx waters was at the end of June 1815 when the *Henry Bell* anchored in Ramsey Bay. The 30-ton *Triton* provided the first regular winter service in 1825, sailing once a week between Whitehaven and Douglas. The first attempt to form a Manx company to operate a steamer service was made in 1826 when Mark Cosnahan, a Manxman living in Liverpool, purchased the new steamer *Victory* and offered shares in her at £50 each. Sadly for the Island, the project came to nothing.

With steam packet vessels such as the *Enterprise* (under the command of Capt. Robert Crawford) maintaining a weekly return service between Liverpool, Ramsey and Greenock and the *St Andrew* sailing between Whitehaven, Douglas and Dublin in addition to numerous individual steam-driven general traders running between Liverpool and Douglas, it was not surprising that merchants and Government officials preferred to use the steamers, using agents or masters of the vessels to forward their mail on arrival in Liverpool. This frequently saved days on delivery.

The result was inevitable and the Post Office were forced to change the port of despatch to Liverpool in 1822 and at the same time Douglas was upgraded to become a Crown Office. The lucrative Liverpool - Isle of Man mail contract was won by the locally-owned St George Steam Packet Co.. They undertook to provide the service for an annual sum of £300 per annum employing different steamers as available and at best rates obtainable. However, the service was still not to the satisfaction of the Manx public.

The 'Manx Advertiser' and the 'Manx Sun' advertised the order of sailings of His Majesty's Royal Mail Packet *St David* for passengers only between Liverpool and Douglas with three return sailings per week boarding without the aid of small boats. Departures from Liverpool were from George's Pierhead and The Quay in Douglas. The Liverpool agents were John Watson of 21 Water Street and the Douglas agent was David Forbes of New Bond Street.

But as with all contractors before, the mail contract was seen as a guaranteed income with the provision of a service as a secondary consideration. As a consequence, several unsuccessful attempts were made to form a Manx shipping company to bring control under the Island and guarantee a reliable service.

The St George Co. placed their older vessels on the route leaving their flagship on the Irish station plying to Dublin. Enough was enough, now there really was a groundswell of public opinion expressing concern that the conduct of mail between the Island and England ought to be under the control of the Island. The only way that this could be achieved was for the Island to have its own steamship company.

Foundation

A meeting was duly called and the minute book from that meeting interestingly enough is titled "Minute book containing the transactions of the Isle of Man Steam Packet Company". The first entry is dated 17th December 1829 and records :–

"Meeting held at Dixon and Steel's saleroom of several inhabitants of Douglas this day for the purpose of establishing a steam packet company, the following resolutions were agreed to:

"The High Bailiff James Quirk was in the chair and a committee of fourteen was appointed to progress the resolutions of the meeting, principal amongst which was to obtain the cost of a suitable steam boat. A sum of £4,500 was subscribed at the meeting which was a considerable sum and indicative of the stature of those present. The committee was immediately set the task of raising the capital to £6,000!

"Matters proceeded quickly and the next meeting held two days later drew up the specification for the vessel with a maximum draft of 8 ft and to be propelled by two 40 hp engines. There was to be accommodation for one hundred passengers, fifty to be cabin class and fifty in the steerage.

The Isle of Man Steam Packet Co. Ltd. Board of Directors 1903
E. J Baldwin, A. W. Moore, D. Maitland, J. T. Cowell, T. Stuttard
W. A. Waid, J. J. Goldsmith

The Isle of Man Steam Packet Co. Ltd. Board of Directors 1910. R. T. Curphey, W. A. Waid, C.T.W. Hughes-Games, W. H. Kitto, D. Maitland, E. J. Baldwin, J. G. Elliott (Chairman)

"Minutes of a meeting on the 22nd December record that quotes for a suitable vessel be sought from a number of shipbuilders. A deputation comprising the High Bailiff, Dr Garrett and Mr Geneste was instructed to "wait upon Lord Strathallen to thank him for his kindness to interfere respecting the mail". Such a tantalising snippet indicates that the Company was already keen to secure the mail contract from the St George Co. It also indicates that the promoters of the Company were no lightweights and the deputation was also instructed to furnish the Governor with details of the proceedings.

"The contract for the vessel was placed with John Wood of Glasgow and at a meeting in Douglas on 6th April 1830 two names were put forward for the vessel – Princess Victoria *and* Mona's Isle *– the latter being chosen by a 31 vote majority."*

The 'Manx Sun' of 16th June carried this report from the 'Greenock Advertiser':

"….the launch of a superior steam vessel of 200 tons called Mona's Isle *of Douglas was launched from the building yard of Mr. John Wood, Port Glasgow. She is to be propelled by two engines of superior power now making by Mr. Robert Napier, Vulcan Foundry, Broomeilaw.*

We understand she is owned principally by the Isle of Man and is intended to ply between Douglas and Liverpool with passengers and to be commanded by Captain Robert Crawford late of the steam packet Enterprise *whose skilful management of that vessel is the best pledge of the judiciousness of his appointment to the* Mona's Isle*……"*

At the time of the launch the vessel was under the command of Capt. Crawford but he resigned on 17th July. Two days later Capt. William Gill, Master of the *Douglas Trader* was appointed Commander of the *Mona's Isle* on an annual salary of £100. The vessel arrived at Douglas on 15th August 1830 and after an inaugural trip to Castletown, Port St Mary and the Calf, she then entered service on the Liverpool route in direct competition with the St George Company.

The 'Manx Sun' carried an advert for the trip which seems to indicate that the vessel was late coming to the Island – were there some pre-delivery problems which were not recorded?

MONA'S ISLE - Steam Packet

Mona's Isle will sail from Douglas to the Menai Bridge and Bangor on Thursday 5th August at eleven o'clock returning the following evening. Fare for the voyage 20s.

An opportunity is thus afforded to the inhabitants of the Island of visiting that stupendous and interesting work. As the present trip is only preparatory to her taking her station between this port and Liverpool, the same excursion will not likely be repeated this season

The advertisement also announced that 'parcels will be carefully forwarded.' The agents were Edward Moore of Douglas and Mark Quayle jun. of 15 Nova Scotia, Liverpool and the Mona's Isle Steam Packet Office is shown as Pier, Douglas.

The many battles that raged between the two rival companies are legend and eventually the flagship of the St George Co., the *St George* was placed on the Liverpool station. It was to be the undoing of the company; disaster came in the form of a south easterly gale and the vessel which had remained at anchor in Douglas Bay dragged her anchor and was wrecked on St Mary's Isle - or Conister Rock as it is more popularly known today. Meanwhile Capt. Gill, who was perhaps more aware of the exposed position of the bay, had taken the *Mona's Isle* to sea to ride out the storm.

The master and crew of the *St George* were rescued in what has become one of the most famous rescues in the early years of the lifeboat service. It was as a direct consequence of this disaster that the Tower of Refuge was built on the rock now such a familiar landmark in Douglas Bay. At that time it was well outside the harbour at Douglas which was still tidal.

A change of name and a contract secured

The loss of the *St George* meant that the Manx company now had the upper hand but the mail contract remained with the St George Co., whose vessels were inferior to the *Mona's Isle*. Much acrimonious correspondence passed between the two companies and their agents with the Mona's Isle Steam Packet Co repeatedly asking the St George Co to transfer the mail contract to them.

In March 1831, in desperation, the Company reluctantly wrote to Sir Francis Peeling, Secretary to the Royal Mail, requesting the transfer of the mail contract, perhaps realising that they had been negotiating with the wrong party. Sir Francis did not reply perhaps indicating that the Post Office was still smarting from their earlier disputes with the Island and the Steam Packet Company.

Business for the new Company grew steadily so much so that in the same month they resolved to purchase or charter a new vessel. In the event they decided on the latter course and appointed Capt

Peter Milligan as its commander at a salary of £84, the ship to be named *Mona*.

The mail contract was eventually transferred later that year to the Mona's Isle Steamship Co. by which name the Company was known although by September 1831 the Company had styled itself as the Isle of Man Steam Packet Co. and all of its assets transferred by February 1832. It was still the same shareholders and Directors – nothing had changed only the name under which the Company operated.

Now with two ships and the mail contract secured, the Company resolved to commence services between Whitehaven and Dublin in addition to the Liverpool route. An outbreak of cholera in Dublin and quarantine restrictions imposed on all vessels plying between Dublin and Liverpool caused the Company to withdraw the Dublin service in April, just one month after it started. The Island did not escape the cholera epidemic and more than 200 people died as a result.

Despite this, the Company continued to expand its business. Now with increased carrying capacity it embarked on excursion traffic, the *Mona's Isle* running an excursion to Menai Bridge and the *Mona* running additional trips to Whitehaven, Kirkcudbright and Garliestown. The Liverpool agent Mark Quayle meanwhile was engaged with the Post Office negotiating a revised contract for the Company, being instructed on 22nd May 1833 to submit a formal tender for the mail contract of £700. After further negotiation, the contract was finalised in July for a twice weekly service for a fee of £850.

On the Island the Post Office had done little to improve the internal distribution of mail to the annoyance of the Bishop and the Garrison commander at Castletown. As a result of continued pressure, the Royal Mail placed contracts with local contractors for additional mail services between Liverpool and Ramsey and Liverpool and Castletown for £100 per annum.

In 1830 the manorial rights of the fourth Duke of Atholl were sold to the Crown and whilst this may not seem to have any significance to the story of the Steam Packet Co. it probably had influenced those who were behind its formation. It certainly was to affect the smuggling trade as the British Treasury were quick to collect the dues and mineral royalties.

For example in February 1833, the *Mona's Isle* was detained by HM Customs necessitating the *Mona* being transferred from the

The Isle of Man Steam Packet Co. Ltd. Board of Directors 1930 Left to Right: W.H.Kitto, G.Fred Clucas, W.H.Dodd, C.T.W. Hughes-Games (Chairman), J.B.Waddington, E.Gordon Thin, A.H. Teare and W.G. Barwell (General Manager)

The Isle of Man Steam Packet Co. Ltd. Board of Directors 1947.

Whitehaven service to convey the mail to Liverpool. The *Mona* was involved later in the year with smuggling spirits from Dublin. As a consequence, stewards were dismissed and a directive issued to Captains to ensure that such practice ceased. It was a problem that was to persist, occupying much of the Directors' time and on occasion, even disrupting the mail service.

The Steam Packet Co. did not have matters all their own way and in 1837 had to deal with a complaint made by former Directors of the company that they were not providing a satisfactory service and that mail was being mishandled. The Company were forced to write a memo to Lord Lichfield, His Majesty's Postmaster General, maintaining that not only were they complying with their contract but exceeding it by providing a daily service for no extra remuneration.

This was supported by another memorandum to the Postmaster General from Governor Ready and signed by forty other dignitaries including the Speaker of the House of Keys, the Deemsters, Customs Officers, the High Bailiff and the Vicar General. Nothing further was heard!

In 1845 the Liverpool agent reported to the Directors that he had been approached by a Post Office Inspector concerning the

The Isle of Man Steam Packet Co. Ltd. Board of Directors 1980 W. Gilbey, F. Kissack, K. Rae, S. Shimmin, A. Alexander, Major Brownsdon, K. Cowley

renewal of the mail contract. At the same time the steamer *Ben my Chree* was to become the mail steamer on the Liverpool run.

On 16th September 1850 the Directors received a letter from the Admiralty strangely still addressed to the Mona's Isle Steam Co.!

"….I am directed by My Lords Commissioners of the Admiralty to acquaint you that from and on the 1st October next the steam vessel conveying the mails under your contract between Liverpool and the Isle of Man is to leave Liverpool at 8am and Douglas at 10am instead of the present hours."

The Directors responded stating that it was not in their interests to change their times due to the convenience of their passengers and the tides at Douglas. The outcome was that the Steam Packet threatened to retreat to the conditions of their contract. Matters rumbled on and even the Governor and the Bishop were complaining about the frequency of the mail.

The Company tabled proposals that they would contract for three mails per week for £1,700 per annum or four mails for £2,500 per annum. The absence of any letter books from the period and scant reference in the minutes leaves a tantalising gap in the continuing battle between the Company, the Admiralty and the Post Office.

The status quo remained until July 1860 when the Directors reported to the half yearly meeting of shareholders that negotiations for a daily mail service had been under consideration by the Postmaster General for sometime – the Directors declining to leave Liverpool at an earlier hour than half past eleven as this would be ruinous to the passenger trade.

How things had changed!

Ramsey and a rival service

In 1861 the ailing Ramsey Steam Packet Co. eventually succumbed and the Isle of Man Steam Packet, anxious to keep the goodwill of Ramsey people, undertook to provide a weekly mail service previously maintained by the Ramsey company's vessel *Manx Fairy*. The contract was passed to the Steam Packet with the approval of the Post Office. The Steam Packet Co. purchased their premises and other quayside assets which guaranteed their presence in Ramsey until services were withdrawn in 1973.

In 1863 the newly appointed Governor Henry Brougham Loch

(later Lord Loch and High Commissioner of South Africa), who proved to be a very active influence over events within the Island, saw the need for a guaranteed daily mail service to the Island and took the matter up once again with the Post Office. They promised to re-open negotiations with the Steam Packet Co. who immediately increased their valuation of the contract to £3,000 per annum – the Post Office walked away.

From reference to the annual accounts of the Company, it would appear that the mail contract remained at the annual fee of £900 per annum. However, in 1879 Governor Loch was part of a deputation from the Island who went to London to meet with Treasury Officials as a result of which the Postmaster General was authorised to accept an offer from the Isle of Man Steam Packet Company to carry out a mail service between Liverpool and Douglas six days a week throughout the year for the annual sum of £4,500 per annum, nearly four times the existing fee!

The Steam Packet had won but the reason was deeply embedded in unrelated battles with the British Treasury and it was only Governor Loch's determination that saw the way through the entrenched views of both sides. It had taken all his drive and diplomatic skills and now at last the Island had got what it had wanted for so long - a daily despatch of mail to and from the Isle of Man and Liverpool.

It was also during this time that the low water landing pier was built at Douglas. It was suggested to the Governor that the pier be named Loch Pier in his honour but this was declined. In 1872 he unveiled the Victoria Pier alongside which vessels could land at all states of the tide. The implication for the mail was that instead of the risky operation of transferring it at low water by small boat, it would be discharged directly to the post carts from the steamer.

In 1883, a parcels service was introduced and by 1886 the Company had introduced a midnight steamer from Douglas to Liverpool into their timetable for the conveyance of mail. Two years later, and still trying to find a quicker way of getting mail to London, the Company carried mail to Holyhead to connect with the Irish Mail train.

Although there was a significant improvement in the timing of the inward mail the venture did not prove profitable as Liverpool was the preferred destination for passengers and still more profitable than the mail. To make things more difficult, the Company had to deal with the Isle of Man, Liverpool and Manchester Steam Ship

The Isle of Man Steam Packet Co. Ltd. Board of Directors 2003. John Watt (Planning & Development Manager and not a board member), Walter Gilbey, Robert Quayle, David Benson (Sea Containers), Dursley Stott, Douglas Grant (Finance Manager not board member), Mark Woodward (Chief Operations Manager not board member) Front row seated: Juan Kelly CBE (Chairman), James B Sherwood (President Seaco), Hamish Ross (Managing Director)

Co. more usually known as the Manx Line which was operating in direct competition on the Liverpool route.

By a strange twist of fate Spencer Walpole, who followed Loch as Lieut. Governor in 1882, became Permanent Secretary to the General Post Office in London after an eleven year term of office. Now there would be no excuse for the Post Office failing to know about the problems of the Isle of Man.

Relations with the Post Office became so cordial that it was not unknown for the departure of the mail packet to be delayed if there had been problems with collections from within the Island. However, as the Steam Packet business continued to expand, it became necessary to increase the Liverpool sailings and two departures were introduced. The first was too early for the mail arriving from London and the second too late - once again the conflict of interests raised its head. The Company now suffering the wrath of businesses which were receiving their London mail twenty-four hours late in the summer period!

The Isle of Man Steam Packet Co. Ltd. Board of Directors 2004. Back Row standing left to right: Douglas Grant (Finance) Dursley Stott, Mark Woodward (Operations), Gill Gawne (Secretary), John Watt (Strategy & Planning) Stuart Garrett (Human Resources), Robert Quayle. Seated: Walter Gilbey, Hamish Ross (MD), Juan Kelly CBE (Chairman), Simon Pooler (Montagu), Peter Longinotti (Montagu)

Unchallenged

The conveyance of mail with the IOM Steam Packet Co. remained unchallenged until 1934 when the advent of air travel became a reality. An airmail service was introduced by the Post Office with a contract awarded to Railway Air Services and 797 letters were carried on the first flight using a DH84 De Havilland Dragon. Other airlines followed and the Post Office was not slow to realise the advantages in time saved and in 1937 the Liverpool mail contract was awarded to Blackpool and West Coast Air Services.

The Steam Packet was left with the parcels traffic but in an effort to keep its interest in the mail contract eventually became part of a syndicate which formed Isle of Man Air Services Ltd and handled the mail contract until taken over by BEA in 1947. Notwithstanding the Company's foray into air traffic, mail was still handled by their vessels which maintained a daily service under the terms of their existing contract.

Despite the advent of regular air services between the Island and the UK, the bulk of the mail throughout the war years and after was carried by the Steam Packet vessels with Royal Mail vans being a familiar sight on the pier awaiting the arrival of the steamer. All the vessels were fitted with locked mail rooms for the conveyance of the mail bags.

The post-war passenger vessels had a mail room located on the Main Deck behind the Third Class bar fitted with a Chubb security lock. A key was held at Liverpool sorting office and another at Douglas. Eventually the mail room was not big enough for all the mail being carried and a slatted wooden locker was built on the same deck against the engine casing for the additional mail bags.

The problem with the air services during the 50's and 60's was that mail was carried on regular passenger aircraft and the capacity was severely limited by both size and weight to something in the order of 30 – 40 bags. Whereas the Steam Packet offered no restriction with the average amount of mail carried being 70 - 80 bags plus parcels. The letters went by van to Regent Street where the sorting office was located at the rear of the General Post Office. A second van took the parcels to a separate sorting facility in Castle Mona Avenue.

Under the terms of the mail contract, which was between Royal Mail and the Steam Packet, the Company undertook to load and unload the mail from the vans to the vessel and convey it between Liverpool and Douglas. Securing the mail in the lockers on board was the responsibility of the senior postman who accompanied the mail and supervised its loading.

Carrying heavy mail bags from the locker up to the Shelter Deck and then up the steps on the pier was no mean feat, particularly at low water. It was not unknown for loose parcels to have to be retrieved by boat hook on the rare occasion! The biggest traffic carried by Royal Mail at this time was boxed kippers outward from Douglas with as many as ten vans taking them to the boat. Such was the amount of summer traffic for this one item that two special vans were brought over from Liverpool by Royal Mail to cope with the collection each season.

With the advent of the first car ferries, dedicated mail rooms were once again incorporated as a direct consequence of high value bags containing money having been lost in the Great Train Robbery, although parcels were carried separately on the Car Deck.

In 1973 the Isle of Man set up its own postal administration, continuing to use Royal Mail as its UK carrier and at the same time undertaking to deliver their mail on the Island. To all intents and purposes there was no real difference with the mail operation and the contract which the Company had remained with Royal Mail.

Ben-my-Chree (Barry Edwards)

The Royal Mail pennant was always hoisted at the foremast by the vessel carrying mail on entering port which gave the Mail Packet preference on entering. When both ports were busy with seasonal traffic, it guaranteed berthing preference to the vessel carrying the mail. This practice continued until the merger with Sealink Manx Line in 1985 which coincided with the move away from Liverpool.

Heysham

Mail was now conveyed in containers by road from Liverpool for despatch from Heysham. After 153 years of the conveyance of mail to the Island it had almost come full circle, the mail originally being despatched to the Island from Whitehaven no more than 40 miles from Heysham.

This move away from Liverpool saw the loss to the Company almost entirely of letter mail and dedicated aircraft were introduced to convey letters to and from the Island. Parcels however continued to be carried by sea and were conveyed by road from Liverpool to Heysham and loaded as unaccompanied trailers. On arrival at Douglas they were taken by Steam Packet vehicles to their former cargo warehouse which the Isle of Man Postal Authority had now leased, where they were sorted and delivered.

In 1995 the IOM Postal Authority completed a new Sorting Office at Spring Valley Industrial Estate with modern letter sorting facilities and a purpose built parcel handling section. A new contract between the Royal Mail and the Steam Packet was drawn up to guarantee loading times for purpose built Royal Mail Parcel Force drop trailers carrying general and priority parcels traffic.

The IOMSP Co. continues to carry mixed mail, letters and parcels, daily to and from the Island with collection and deliveries timed to match the sailing schedules, maintaining the long unbroken connection with Royal Mail since 1832.

CHAPTER TWO

THE EARLY YEARS 1830-1899

Following the formation of the Company, a total of £7,250 was subscribed in 290 shares of £25 and the Company's first steamer was launched from the yard of John Wood, Glasgow on 30th June 1830 and named *Mona's Isle*. The new ship inaugurated the Douglas and Liverpool service on 17th August 1830 carrying 15 saloon and 17 steerage passengers. There was fierce competition with the St George Steam Packet Company's *St. George* until that vessel was wrecked on Conister Rock in Douglas Bay in an easterly gale on 20th November 1830.

On 11th July 1831 the Postmaster General awarded the mail contract to the new Isle of Man Steam Packet Company. The mails had to be carried twice weekly in summer and once weekly during the winter for a sum of £1,000 per annum.

In 1832 a second vessel was ordered from John Wood of Glasgow and a small steamer called the *Mona* entered service in July of that year. She was slightly faster than the 'Isle' and usually crossed between Douglas and Liverpool in seven-and-a-half hours.

The third wooden paddle steamer in the fleet, the *Queen of the Isle*, was completed in 1834. A daily sailing (Sundays excepted) operated that summer, leaving Liverpool at 10.00 and Douglas at 08.00.

A rival Manx company styled the Isle of Man and Liverpool Steam Navigation Company ordered a 300-ton steamer from Steele

The Company's first vessel was the wooden-hulled paddle steamer **Mona's Isle** (1). She was built at Port Glasgow in 1830 and entered service between Douglas and Liverpool on 16th August that year. *(IOMSP Co Ltd collection)*

of Greenock in 1835. She was called the *Monarch* and lasted until the new company collapsed in 1837.

The final wooden steamer in the fleet, the *King Orry* [1] was also the only vessel to be built in the Isle of Man at John Winram's yard at Douglas. The hull was launched on 10th February 1842 and the *Mona's Isle* then towed it to Napier's works at Glasgow for the engines to be installed.

The first iron ship in the Steam Packet fleet was launched on 3rd May 1845 from Robert Napier's yard and was named *Ben-my-Chree* [1]. A second iron paddle steamer was launched by Napier on 28th April 1846 and named *Tynwald* [1]. She was nearly double the size of any of her predecessors and was built to cope with the rapidly increasing traffic. The *Tynwald* had the dubious distinction of being the first Steam Packet vessel whose launch was delayed by a strike in the shipbuilding yard.

The Company's pioneer steamer, the *Mona's Isle*, continued to sail throughout the 1840s, although the Directors had advertised her for sale from 1837. She was reboiled by Napier for £500 in 1845. The pioneer vessel was finally sold for demolition in 1851 for the sum of £580.

The Company was experimenting with new routes and in 1842 commenced sailings to Fleetwood. These continued on a spasmodic and intermittent basis over the next 34 years until a regular summer service was established in 1876.

The **Mona** (I) was the Company's second ship and became a Liverpool tug after her retirement in 1841. *(Manx Museum)*

The **Queen of the Isle** served with the Company for ten years between 1834 and 1844. *(Ferry Publications Library)*

J. & G. Thomson of Govan launched the *Mona's Queen* [1] on 27th November 1852 and the new ship achieved 13.02 knots on trials. In September 1853 the 'Queen' made a special trip to Dublin with Steam Packet shareholders as passengers to enable them to see Queen Victoria on her visit to the Irish capital.

The Isle of Man Steam Packet Company experienced some competition from 1853 until 1861. A local Ramsey company in the north of the Island built the *Manx Fairy* in 1853 and the following year a group of Castletown (in the south) businessmen built the

Ellan Vannin. The Castletown venture collapsed in 1857 but the *Manx Fairy* remained on the Ramsey station until 1861.

The Prince's Landing Stage at Liverpool was opened on 1st September 1857 and generated an upsurge in passenger traffic. Passengers could now directly board the Douglas-bound steamer without the delays and inconvenience involved in either being rowed out to a vessel anchored in mid-river, or awaiting the tide to leave the enclosed dock system.

In 1858 Robert Napier took the *King Orry* [1] in part payment of

The **Mona's Queen** (I) was launched in 1853 remained in the fleet until 1880. *(Manx Museum)*

The first **King Orry** was built in Douglas in 1842 but was taken Napier's shipyard in part payment for the **Douglas** (I).

The iron-hulled **Ben-my-Chree** (1) is seen leaving Douglas. She entered service in 1845 and was fitted with the engines from the **Queen of the Isle**. *(Stan Basnett collection)*

The **Tynwald** (1) followed the first 'Ben' into service in 1846 and served for twenty years with the Company. *(Manx Museum)*

The **Snaefell** (1) was a product of Caird & Co. of Greenock. She was sold on to the Zeeland Steamship Company in 1875. *(Manx Museum)*

new construction. The sum of £5,000 was allowed against the cost of the new *Douglas* which was launched at Glasgow on 28th May 1858. The *Douglas* achieved a trials speed of 17.25 knots which reputedly made her the fastest steamship built to date, and she reduced the time for the Liverpool and Douglas passage to between four-and-a-half and five hours.

With the outbreak of the American Civil War, the Confederate Government acquired many fast paddle steamers to run the Federal blockade, and in November 1862 the Steam Packet Company sold the *Douglas* for £24,000 to the Confederate agents Fraser, Trenholm & Company. The steamer sailed to Charleston where she was renamed *Margaret & Jessie* but on her tenth run to beat the blockade of the southern ports, she was captured by the Federal warship *Nansemond* on 5th November 1863. The former Manx steamer was taken to New York and fitted out as a gunboat for the Federal Navy being renamed USS *Gettysburg* in May 1864. She remained with the U.S. Navy as a transport and survey vessel until decommissioned and sold in Genoa in May 1879.

In the mid 1860s, three generally similar paddle steamers were launched for the Steam Packet Company from the yard of Caird & Company of Greenock. They were the *Snaefell* [1] in 1863 the *Douglas* [2] in 1864 and the *Tynwald* [2] in 1866.

The difficulties of landing and embarking large numbers of passengers at Douglas were overcome in 1871 with the opening on 1st July of the new Victoria Pier. Initially the pier was a very spartan affair providing two deep-water berths until it was extended to its present length in 1885.

The Steam Packet fleet increased to six ships in 1871 when the *King Orry* [2] was launched by R. Duncan & Company of Glasgow. Four years later the *Ben-my-Chree* [2] was built by the Barrow Shipbuilding Company. The 1,000 gross ton mark was passed for the first time as the new 'Ben' had a gross tonnage of 1,030 but she was a slow vessel capable of only 14 knots, this being two knots slower than her original contract speed.

The new pier at Llandudno opened in May 1877 and provided a deep-water berthing head making it more practical to provide sailings to the Welsh resort.

The supremacy of the paddle steamer was first challenged in the Steam Packet fleet by the completion of the *Mona* [2] in 1878. She was a single-screw steamer launched from Laird Brothers' yard at Birkenhead in May 1878 and attained 12.5 knots on her trials. The

The *Snaefell* (2) at the Steam Packet berth in Ramsey inner harbour, which was tidal. She served the Company from 1876 until 1904. *(Midwood/Stan Basnett collection)*

The *Mona's Isle* (3) on Scarlett Point in 1892. She was stranded for two days before being assisted off the rocks by the *Tynwald* (3). *(Manx Museum)*

Mona was much more economical to run than the paddle steamers and was better suited to the winter service.

The last iron ship and the first twin-screw steamer in the fleet was the *Fenella* [1] launched in June 1881 by the Barrow Shipbuilding Company. However, despite the success of the early screw steamers, the Steam Packet Company ordered a large paddle

17

steamer from Caird & Company of Greenock in 1881. She was named *Mona's Isle* [3] and achieved 18.18 knots on trials.

In 1882 the hull of the *Mona's Isle* [2] was considered sound enough to warrant her conversion to a twin-screw steamer and this work was undertaken by Westray, Copeland & Company at Barrow-in-Furness. Her name was changed to *Ellan Vannin* and she became associated with services from Ramsey.

When the *Mona* [2] was at anchor near the Mersey Bar lightship on 5th August 1883, the Spanish steamer *Rita* ran into her. The *Mona* sank in half an hour and all her crew and two passengers were picked up by the tug *Conqueror*. To replace the sunken vessel the Company ordered the *Peveril* [1] from the Barrow Shipbuilding Company.

During 1884 the *Ben-my-Chree* [2] was reboiled. Two additional funnels were fitted so that she had a total of four: two forward of the paddle boxes and two aft. Although she now looked one of the most impressive vessels which the Steam Packet Company has ever operated, the new boilers did little to increase her slow speed of only 14 knots.

With the entry into service of the *Mona's Queen* [2] in 1885 the Steam Packet fleet increased to ten vessels.

In 1887 a rival concern styled the Isle of Man, Liverpool and Manchester Steamship Company built the paddle steamers *Queen*

A splendid study of the ***Snaefell*** (2) rolling in a stiff breeze as she leaves Ramsey and still flying the 'Blue Peter' from her foremast.
(Southward/Stan Basnett collection)

The ill-fated screw ship ***Ellan Vannin*** was built as the ***Mona's Isle*** (2) in 1860. She sank with all hands at the Mersey Bar in December 1909.
(Manx Museum)

Victoria and *Prince of Wales*. Both these ships were faster by half an hour than any Steam Packet vessel on the Liverpool and Douglas route. Competition became fierce and in 1888 both companies were involved in a price-cutting war. The fares of the Manx Line, as the new company was popularly known, were reduced to 5/- (25p) First Class and 2/6d (12.5p) Second Class. The wholly uneconomic practice of racing was reintroduced with the rival steamers leaving Liverpool or Douglas at identical times. In November 1888 both the *Queen Victoria* and the *Prince of Wales* were sold to the Steam Packet Company. With the acquisition of the two new steamers the *Douglas*

The *Peveril* (1) entered service in 1884, her career being cut short when she was sunk in a collision off Douglas in 1899. She is seen leaving the harbour at Ramsey. *(Stan Basnett collection)*

[2] and the *Tynwald* [2] were effectively redundant and were sold for breaking-up in January 1889.

In 1887 the Steam Packet Company purchased the Imperial Hotel on the quay at Douglas and, until 1969, established its headquarters there. Passenger traffic was on the rapid increase towards the end of the century and 516,359 passengers were carried in 1894. This was an increase of 230,000 on the total of ten years earlier. A spate of opposition companies was encountered in the 1890s but nothing as serious as the Manx Line emerged.

The Diamond Jubilee year of Queen Victoria saw the launch of the magnificent paddle steamer *Empress Queen* from the Fairfield yard at Govan on 14th March 1897. She achieved 21.75 knots on trials and the following year was averaging 3 hours 5 minutes for the Liverpool - Douglas passage.

The *Peveril* [1] sank off Douglas on 17th September 1899 following a collision with the coaster *Monarch*. The *Peveril's* crew and one passenger were transferred to the *Monarch* and were landed at Douglas.

The third **Mona** (3) came third-hand to the Company. Built as the **Calais-Douvres** in 1889 for the London Chatham & Dover Railway's Dover-Calais service, she came to the Steam Packet from Liverpool & Douglas Steamers to whom she had been sold in 1900. She was only to serve for six years before she was broken-up in 1909. *(Jeffrey D. Sankey collection)*

21

The **Ben-my-Chree** (2) was the most distinctive of all Steam Packet ships following her re-boilering in 1884 when she was fitted with two extra funnels. *(Manx Museum)*

The **Fenella** (1) was built at Barrow in 1881and remained in service until 1929. *(Manx Museum)*

The **King Orry** (2) paddling purposefully towards Douglas at the close of a routine voyage from Liverpool. *(Liverpool Maritime Museum)*

The *Tynwald* (2) of 1866 served the Company for 23 years.. It is low water at Douglas as the ship sits at the Red Pier waiting for the tide. *(Ferry Publications Library)*

The *Prince of Wales* was one of a pair of powerful steamers purchased from the rival Liverpool & Manchester SS Co. (Manx Line) in 1888. *(Manx Museum)*

The magnificent *Empress Queen* was the largest and fastest paddle steamer ever built for the Steam Packet and entered service in 1897. A product of the Fairfield yard, she was wrecked on Bembridge Ledge (Isle of Wight) whilst trooping in 1916. *(Manx Museum)*

23

This quite remarkable study of the **Queen Victoria** shows both her energy and elegant lines as she heads into a calm Irish Sea. Built for the Manx Line in 1887, with her sister **Prince of Wales**, she entered Steam Packet Company service in the following year. The stokers are obviously doing a magnificent job! *(Jeffrey D. Sankey collection)*

CHAPTER THREE

THE YEARS OF PLENTY 1900-1913

At the turn of the century, the Isle of Man Steam Packet was operating a fleet of eleven vessels which comprised eight paddle steamers and three twin-screw steamers. The oldest was the *Ellan Vannin* (built as the *Mona's Isle* [2] in 1860), and the newest was the *Empress Queen* of 1897.

Some fairly stiff opposition was being encountered from Liverpool & Douglas Steamers (formed in 1899) and a price-cutting war was in progress. In 1900 a First Class saloon return was available at 4/- (20p).

Until 1901 all the Steam Packet Company's ships had been ordered by and built for the Company, with the exception of the *Queen Victoria* and *Prince of Wales*, purchased from the Manx Line in 1888. However, a replacement was needed for the *Peveril* [1], lost in 1899, and so in 1901 the Company purchased the 813-ton single-screw steamer *Dora* from the London & South Western Railway Company. She was quickly renamed *Douglas* [3].

On 28th June 1902, the Coronation of King Edward VII was marked by a Review of the Fleet at Spithead. On this occasion the *Mona's Isle* [3] was chartered to Lunn's for a special cruise from Southampton Docks.

In December 1902, Liverpool & Douglas Steamers went into liquidation and the following year the Steam Packet Company purchased the former Dover Strait vessel *Calais-Douvres* from the liquidators for £6,000 and renamed her *Mona* [3]. Built in 1889, this vessel became the final paddle steamer to be added to the Manx fleet.

The *Empress Queen* was fitted with Marconi 'wireless' in 1903 and was the first Steam Packet ship to be so equipped. The total number of passengers carried in 1903 amounted to 711,514 and the standard return fare was 10/- (50p).

In 1904 the Isle of Man received its first visit from a steam turbine vessel. The Midland Railway Company's *Londonderry*

Alongside at Ramsey is the steamer **Peveril** (1). Her presence in the harbour has attracted a good crowd of sight-seers. *(Midwood/Stan Basnett collection)*

operated an excursion sailing from the newly- opened port of Heysham on 13th August. Two months prior to this the railway company had launched the turbine steamer *Manxman* and with such a name she was obviously destined to provide a rival service. On 1st June 1905 the *Manxman* inaugurated the service, the afternoon crossing from Heysham to Douglas being scheduled to take just 2 hours 40 minutes.

To counter this opposition, the Isle of Man Steam Packet Company placed an order with Armstrong, Whitworth & Company of Newcastle-upon-Tyne for a new direct- drive turbine steamer which would be guaranteed to steam at least three-quarters of a

25

Top: The *Snaefell* (3) was the first Steam Packet ship to come from Cammell Laird's at Birkenhead and entered service in 1910. She was torpedoed in the Mediterranean eight years later. (*Jeffrey D. Sankey collection*)

Above: The *King Orry* (3) served the Steam Packet from 1913 until her loss during the Dunkirk evacuation in 1940. (*John Clarkson collection*)

Right: The second *Mona's Queen* was the Steam Packet's last operational paddle steamer and finally passed for breaking in 1929. (*John Clarkson collection*)

The **Ben-my-Chree** (3), dressed overall and approaching the Victoria Pier, was to become one of the best-loved of all Manx steamers. (*John Clarkson collection*)

knot faster than the *Manxman*. This was the Steam Packet's first turbine steamer, and the only vessel ever to be built for them on the north-east coast. She was named *Viking* at her launch on 7th March 1905 and on her trials achieved 23.53 knots. The *Viking* became the mainstay of the Douglas - Fleetwood service on which she would burn up to 60 tons of coal a day. On 25th May 1907 she crossed from Fleetwood to Douglas in 2 hours 22 minutes, a record that stood until the introduction of SeaCat services in June 1994.

The success of the *Viking* prompted the Company to order a larger turbine steamer from the Barrow yard of Vickers, Sons & Maxim Limited. She was launched on 23rd March 1908 and named *Ben-my-Chree* [3]. Direct-drive turbines coupled to triple screws gave a trials speed of 24.26 knots. The new 'Ben' had a passenger certificate for 2,549, carried a crew of 119 and could burn 95 tons of coal in one day's steaming. On 9th July 1909 the *Ben-my-Chree* made her fastest recorded passage from Liverpool to Douglas, berth to berth, in 2 hours 57 minutes.

On 3rd December 1909 the *Ellan Vannin* left Ramsey for Liverpool at 01.13 with 15 passengers, 21 crew, mail and 60 tons of cargo. A severe north-westerly gale blew up whilst she was on passage, and as the steamer approached the Mersey Bar lightship at about 06.45 the gale reached storm force. In what was to become the worst peacetime disaster ever to befall the Company, the *Ellan Vannin* foundered between the lightship and the Q.1 buoy at about 07.00. She is believed to have been swept by heavy seas and broached to, sinking by the stern. All aboard were lost. Later the same day lifebuoys, bags of turnips and a piano were seen floating near the Formby lightship but it was not until 8th December that

The splendid *Viking* of 1905 was the Steam Packet's first turbine steamer and served during both World Wars, not passing for scrap until her 49th season. *(IOMSP Co Ltd)*

The magnificent **Ben-my-Chree** (3) on the measured mile prior to entering service in 1908. The 24-knot steamer was tragically a casualty of the Great War. *(Jeffrey D. Sankey collection)*

the first bodies were washed ashore.

The subsequent Board of Trade Enquiry into the disaster had no direct evidence available to form an opinion as to the precise cause. The Enquiry found that the ship was in good order and there were no criticisms of the Company, Master or crew.

On 12th February 1910 the *Snaefell* [3] was launched at Birkenhead. She was the first Steam Packet ship to be built by Cammell Laird & Company (the *Mona* [2] was built by Laird Brothers). The new *Snaefell* was extensively used on the Liverpool to Douglas winter service.

In 1911 the railway-operated Fleetwood overnight steamers *Duke of York* and *Duke of Lancaster* were purchased by Turkish interests and sent to Cammell Laird at Birkenhead for complete refurbishment. The deal with the Turks fell through and the Isle of Man Steam Packet Company purchased both these vessels. The *Duke of Lancaster* was renamed *The Ramsey* and the *Duke of York* became the *Peel Castle*.

A new *King Orry* [3] was launched at Cammell Laird's, Birkenhead on 11th March 1913 to replace the 1871 paddle steamer of the same name. The ship's sponsor, Miss Waid, was rather startled at the launching ceremony when the ship began to move down the slipway before she had finished her speech! This was the first geared turbine steamer in the fleet - these had proved to be more economical than direct-drive.

In 1913, such was the boom in Manx tourism that the total number of passengers carried by the Isle of Man Steam Packet Company rose to 1,152,048. This represented the vast proportion of visitors to the Isle of Man, but the Midland Railway Company's Heysham-Douglas service and the Liverpool & North Wales Steamship Company's Llandudno-Douglas service would have increased the total.

CHAPTER FOUR

THE GREAT WAR 1914-1918

The First World War began on 4th August in what should have been the peak of the Steam Packet Company's summer seasonal traffic. Passenger arrivals over the first weekend in August fell away drastically and at a special meeting of the Directors on 10th August it was decided to lay up the *Ben-my-Chree* [3], the *Viking* and the *Empress Queen* with immediate effect.

By the end of October 1914 the *King Orry*, *Peel Castle*, *The Ramsey* and the *Snaefell* had all been requisitioned by the Admiralty which had also asked for plans of all five of the Company's paddle steamers. From fifteen vessels at the outbreak of the war, the Steam Packet's fleet was reduced to four within a few months. The *Douglas*, *Tynwald*, *Fenella* and *Tyrconnel* remained to maintain the wartime

Robert Lloyd's painting of the **King Orry** (3) shows her at the surrender of the German High Seas Fleet east of the Firth of Forth in November 1918. This event represented one of the Steam Packet's greatest hours. *(By kind permission of Stan Basnett)*

services - they were all small screw steamers, each of under 1,000 tons.

The number of passengers carried in 1914 dropped by almost two-thirds of the 1913 total to just 404,481.

The Steam Packet Company's five paddle steamers and two large turbine steamers were pressed into war service early in 1915. The *Prince of Wales* had her name changed to *Prince Edward* to avoid confusion with the battleship.

The *Viking* and the *Ben-my-Chree* were both converted to carry seaplanes. A hangar was built aft of the second funnel to house six seaplanes which would be lifted in and out of the water by a crane.

There was a once popular story that the 'Ben' was loaded with ammunition and sent round the Cape of Good Hope to service warships that were under orders to sink the German light cruiser *Königsberg* which was sheltering in the River Rufiji in Tanganyika (Tanzania). She is said to have made this long journey, from England to East Africa, at an average speed in excess of 22 knots, including stops for coaling. However, as surviving log fragments have shown, it would have been impossible for her to have made the trip between her North Sea operations and her main Mediterranean war work.

On 7th August 1915 HMS *Ramsey* (ex *The Ramsey*) left Scapa Flow in the Orkney Islands. Next day, when she was in the south-east approach to the Pentland Firth, she challenged a supposedly Russian ship which turned out to be the German minelaying raider *Meteor*. The Ramsey was fired on at short range and sank rapidly with very heavy loss of life after a torpedo from the *Meteor* had shattered her stern. Fifty-two of the *Ramsey's* crew were killed, and forty-six were picked up by the raider.

The *King Orry* struck a submerged reef in the Sound of Islay when she was steaming at 19 knots on 9th June 1915. Using the hand steering gear, and with only the port turbines working, she

The *Viking* became the seaplane carrier HMS *Vindex* during the First World War. *(Imperial War Museum)*

The *Peel Castle* was built as the Lancashire & Yorkshire Railway's *Duke of York* in 1894 and was purchased by the Steam Packet in 1912. *(Imperial War Museum)*

proceeded to Birkenhead for repairs by Cammell Laird.

At Easter 1916 the *Tynwald* [3] made trooping trips to Kingstown (Dun Laoghaire) in connection with the suppression of the Irish rebellion.

Whilst inward bound to Southampton from Le Havre at 05.00 on 1st February 1916, the *Empress Queen* stranded on Bembridge Ledge, Isle of Wight. Visibility was only a few metres with light airs and a smooth sea. She ran aground on a rising tide and the 1,300

troops on board were taken off by destroyers. It was not expected to be a difficult job to tow her off but, after several attempts had failed, a severe gale blew up and she became a total loss.

On 11th January 1917 the *Ben-my-Chree* was anchored in a supposedly safe bay off the island of Castellorizo (off the south-west Mediterranean coast of Turkey). However, the surrounding hills were occupied by Turks who opened fire, igniting petrol and holing the ship which sank in shallow water. The 'Ben' was

During the First World War the *King Orry* (3) served as an armed boarding vessel at Scapa Flow. *(Imperial War Museum)*

The *Snaefell* (3) on Admiralty duties prior to her loss in June 1918. *(Imperial War Museum)*

The **Mona's Queen** (2) in full dazzle paint and berthed in Weymouth Harbour during the First World War. *(John Clarkson collection)*

abandoned after half an hour, and her crew of 250 were able to get safely ashore with only four wounded. The Master and the Chief Engineer later returned to the 'Ben' and saved the ship's cat and two dogs.

On 6th February 1917 the *Mona's Queen* [2] left Southampton under the command of Captain Cain with 1,000 troops on board, bound for Le Havre. Some twenty miles from the French coast a German U-Boat surfaced almost dead ahead. The 'Queen' kept on course, despite a torpedo being fired at her, and the U-Boat's conning tower was struck by her port paddle-box, the steel paddle floats inflicting severe damage. Despite diving immediately the U-Boat (UC.26) was not fatally wounded and arrived at Ostend two days later for repairs and overhaul. UC.26 was finally sunk in the Thames estuary by the Royal Navy on 30th April 1917.

The *Mona's Queen* was disabled by the incident but managed to

steam slowly into Le Havre. After discharging her troops she steamed back to Southampton for repairs at Harland & Wolff and resumed her trooping duties on 17th March.

The *King Orry* [3] had the distinction of following the light cruiser HMS *Cardiff* and 14 German capital ships at the surrender of the German High Seas Fleet, forty miles east of the Island of May at the entrance to the Firth of Forth, on 21st November 1918.

In December 1918 the Isle of Man Steam Packet Company's fleet consisted of the *Fenella* [1], *Tynwald* [3] and *Douglas* [3] available for service, and the *Mona's Queen* [2], *Peel Castle* and *King Orry* [3] under requisition, in addition to the cargo steamer *Tyrconnel*. The two principal passenger carriers the *Ben-my-Chree* [3] and the *Empress Queen* had been lost, as had the *Snaefell* [3] and *The Ramsey*. The *Prince of Wales* and the *Queen Victoria* were not worth reconditioning, nor was the *Mona's Isle* [3]. The *Viking* was purchased back from the Admiralty.

CHAPTER FIVE

THE INTER-WAR YEARS 1919-1939

An unusual and important problem faced the Isle of Man Steam Packet Company at the end of the war. The fleet of steamers was dispersed and could only be brought back to pre-war standards at considerable cost. In February 1919 the Company had a capital of £200,000 in £1 shares and had more than £700,000 in investments, plus a fleet which had been written down to a book value of under £70,000. The Company had received more than £500,000 from chartering fees, payments for loss of steamers and awards from underwriters.

At the Company's Annual General Meeting some of the Directors argued that it would be perfectly possible to wind up the Company if the shareholders so wished, and £5 could be paid out for every £1 of the issued capital. A group of shareholders did in fact propose that the Directors should either offer to sell the Company to the Manx Government or dispose of it as a going concern. The Chairman led a counter-attack and proposed that the Company should carry on, this proposal being approved.

The fleet in 1919 had a total passenger capacity of less than 10,000: in 1914 this figure was in excess of 20,000. Yet with the return of the holiday trade in 1919, incoming passenger arrivals were 343,332.

The Company started to replace the depleted fleet by purchasing the *Hazel* from the Laird Line in January 1919. She had been built at Govan in 1907 for the Ardrossan - Portrush service which was not restarted after the war. The *Hazel* was renamed *Mona* [4].

The *Mona's Queen* [2] was refitted by Cammell Laird in April 1919 and was available for the summer season. The *King Orry* [3] had a period of trooping between Southampton and French ports but returned to Cammell Laird early in 1919 for complete refurbishment and was back on Steam Packet service in July. The *Peel Castle* sailed as a troopship until May 1919 after which she was returned to the Company.

In order to boost the passenger capacity of the fleet for the 1919 summer season the elderly paddle steamer *La Marguerite* was chartered from the Liverpool & North Wales Steamship Company from 28th June to 16th September. With her passenger certificate for 2,077 she was extensively used for the period of the charter.

The Isle of Man Steam Packet Company purchased the Midland Railway Company's turbine steamer *Manxman* from the Admiralty and sent her to Barrow for a complete refit in February 1920. In an attempt to replace the *Ben-my-Chree* [3], lost in 1917, the *Manxman* was placed on the principal Liverpool - Douglas route. The *Viking*, which had survived the war, was back on the Fleetwood

This photograph taken from the Peveril Hotel shows the Victoria Pier and the building affectionately known as 'The Triangle' with its ornate clock tower. It was replaced by the present terminal building in 1961. (Manx Museum)

35

Top: The *King Orry* (3) became something of a tourist attraction after she had run aground at New Brighton in August 1921. *(John Clarkson collection)*

Above: The *Manx Maid* (1) was purchased by the Steam Packet in 1923 having previously been the Channel Islands steamer *Caesarea* of 1910. *(John Clarkson collection)*

Right: The *Mona's Isle* (4) was the second Dover-based vessel to transfer to the Steam Packet. Built at Dumbarton as the *Onward* in 1905, the turbine steamer was purchased in 1920. *(John Clarkson collection)*

The new 'Ben' is seen on official speed trials in the Firth of Clyde and looks every inch a flier. *(Wirral Archives)*

The launch of the new flagship ***Ben-my-Chree*** (4) at Birkenhead in 1927 began a remarkable career. She was such a popular ship that many Fleet
Commodores preferred her to the Company's centenary steamer, the ***Lady of Mann*** (1). *(Wirral Archives)*

The *Manxman* was another inter-war purchase. She was built for the Midland Railway's new Heysham services in 1904 and was a regular visitor to Douglas. She eventually passed to the Steam Packet in 1920 without a change of name. *(John Clarkson collection)*

After the war the *Peel Castle* was recommissioned and served the Company until 1939. *(Bruce Peter collection)*

Douglas service in June 1920.

Another purchase of second-hand tonnage was made in March 1920 when the Company bought the *Viper* from G. & J. Burns of Glasgow. She had been built in 1906 for the Ardrossan - Belfast daylight service and was renamed *Snaefell* [4] for her Manx service.

A third purchase was made in 1920 when the 1905-built Dover Strait steamer *Onward* was acquired. Her name was eventually changed to *Mona's Isle* [4].

In 1920 the Steam Packet Company's fleet carried a total of 1,094,220 passengers. This fleet was a rather motley collection of thirteen vessels and there was no 'crack' ship. Only five had been built for the Company, the remaining eight having been brought in second-hand. Just one paddle steamer remained - the *Mona's Queen* [2] of 1885, and it was an elderly fleet with an average age of 22 years. This state of affairs was set to continue for almost a decade until the Company's new building programme commenced with the *Ben-my-Chree* [4] of 1927.

The salvage steamer *Valette* raised the wreck of the *Ben-my-Chree*

The **Rushen Castle** was originally the Lancashire & Yorkshire Railway's **Duke of Cornwall** of 1898. The Steam Packet purchased her in 1928 and she survived in Manx service until 1946. *(John Clarkson collection)*

The Company's centenary ship the **Lady of Mann** (1) going down the ways at Barrow in March 1930. *(Jeffrey D.Sankey)*

The **Ramsey Town** was originally the Midland Railway's steamer *Antrim*. The Steam Packet acquired her in 1928. *(John Clarkson collection)*

[3] at Castellorizo in 1920 and the hulk was towed to Piraeus. Following examination, repairs were not considered possible.

In 1921 the *Manxman*'s boilers were adapted for burning oil fuel which enabled her to keep sailing throughout the coal strike of 1926. She was the first Steam Packet ship to be so treated.

In November 1923 the Company made another second-hand purchase when it bought the Southampton-based *Caesarea* from the Southern Railway Company. Earlier that year the vessel had struck rocks off St Helier, Jersey. The Steam Packet Company arranged for her to be towed to Barrow for refurbishment and she was converted to burn oil fuel. The *Caesarea* was renamed *Manx Maid* [1] and commenced on the Company's sailings in Summer 1924.

The major strikes of 1926 disrupted the Steam Packet's operations. The coal-burning units all had empty bunkers and passenger arrivals at Douglas slumped by 156,000. The main Liverpool - Douglas route was maintained by the two oil-burners *Manxman* and *Manx Maid*. From 20th May 1926 sailings between Liverpool and Douglas were reduced to a single passage each way daily.

The new *Ben-my-Chree* [4] was launched by Cammell Laird at Birkenhead on 5th April 1927. Construction had been rapid - the keel had been laid just over four months earlier in November 1926. Cammell Laird had been promised a bonus of £2,000 if they could meet the delivery date of 25th June 1927. The new 'Ben' achieved 22.8 knots on her trials and her passenger capacity was for 2,586, by a coincidence the same figure as her gross tonnage. In July 1927 Cammell Laird reported a loss of £17,000 on building the 'Ben'. The Steam Packet paid £192,000 and then agreed to round up the figure to £200,000. The 'Ben' was the Company's first new ship since 1913 and the first to be built as an oil-burner.

In 1928 the Steam Packet Company took over the Heysham - Douglas service from the Midland Railway Company and had a virtual monopoly of the Manx passenger traffic for the next 41 years. Two vessels were purchased from the railway company: the *Duke of Cornwall* of 1898 which was renamed *Rushen Castle*, and the *Antrim* of 1904 which was renamed *Ramsey Town*.

A third additional steamer was added to the fleet in 1928. She was the Southern Railway Company's *Victoria* built in 1907 and was a younger sister of the *Mona's Isle* [4], ex *Onward*. The *Victoria* retained her original name throughout her Steam Packet service.

The Isle of Man Steam Packet Company's fleet in 1928

The ***Mona's Queen*** (3) under construction at Cammell Laird's. This bird's-eye view gives a good impression of the ship's layout and her long, lean hull. *(Wirral Archives)*

The **Ben-my-Chree**'s (4) hull was painted white in 1932 after the Board decided it would improve the image of the Company. *(John Clarkson collection)*

The First Class Dining Room on the *Mona's Queen* (3) was situated forward on the extra Forecastle Deck which must have been an uncomfortable place to eat in any weather. *(Wirral Archives)*

consisted of seventeen steamers. At one end of the scale the new 'crack' steamer *Ben-my-Chree* was just one year old, whilst at the other end of the scale the *Fenella* [1] was still steaming after 47 years. The total age of the fleet amounted to 440 years, giving an average age of 26 years, four more than in 1920. The last paddle steamer, the *Mona's Queen* [2] of 1885, remained in service.

A specially designed cargo vessel was launched from Cammell Laird's yard in 1929 and named *Peveril* [2]. Early on in her career she was passing through the Brunswick Lock at Liverpool when the swing bridge operated prematurely and removed her mainmast! The end of the 1929 summer season turned out to be a time for farewells. The Company's last paddle steamer, the *Mona's Queen* [2], made her final passenger sailing from Fleetwood to Douglas; the *Fenella* [1] completed her last voyage from Workington to Douglas and the *Tynwald* [3], after spending the summer operating cruises from Blackpool's North Pier, was laid up at Barrow. The number of passengers carried on the Company's steamers in 1929 totalled 1,177,799.

On 3rd July 1929 the Company placed an order with the newly-formed shipbuilding company Vickers-Armstrong Limited at

The *Victoria* of 1907 was a sister of the *Onward/Mona's Isle* (4) and joined the Steam Packet from the Southern Railway in 1928. Converted to oil burning later in her career, this remarkable vessel saw 49 years' service and was not broken up until her fiftieth. She was the Steam Packet's last two-funnelled steamer in service. *(Bruce Peter collection)*

Barrow for a new passenger steamer. She was launched as the *Lady of Mann* on 4th March to celebrate the centenary of the Isle of Man Steam Packet Company. In her first years of service the 'Lady' had a passenger certificate for 2,873.

In the spring of 1932 the *Ben-my-Chree* was chartered to take a sailing to the Eucharistic Conference being held in Dublin and it was thought appropriate to paint her hull white for the occasion. For the sum of just £63, Vickers-Armstrong carried out this work. The 'Ben's' white hull was very favourably received and the *Lady of Mann* was painted white in time for the 1933 summer season.

The Steam Packet Company returned to Cammell Laird at Birkenhead for its next new steamer and the *Mona's Queen* [3] was launched in April 1934 with a white hull and green boot topping. In the 'Ben' of 1927, the 'Lady' of 1930 and the new 'Queen', the Company had perhaps the finest short-sea ships in the world, as well as offering a service second-to-none.

In March 1936 two new vessels were ordered from Vickers-Armstrong at Barrow. A double launch took place on 16th December 1936 when the *Fenella* [2] and the *Tynwald* [4] entered the water. The new ships were specifically designed for the winter services and were the forerunners of the 1946 'King Orry class'which were so familiar until the early 1980s. Although turbine steamers, both the new ships were given squat funnels with horizontal tops which were the fashion of the new motor ships of the 1930s but which, in the view of this writer, greatly detracted from their otherwise fine lines.

In March 1937 the Manx Government grudgingly agreed to Sunday excursionists and the new *Tynwald* inaugurated special Sunday sailings. In the summer of 1937 the Isle of Man Steam Packet Company was operating a total of eighteen steamers, the highest number in its history and a fleet total never to be exceeded.

The *King Orry* was converted to burn oil fuel in time for the 1939 summer season. In that final summer before the outbreak of war, the *Ben-my-Chree* was rostered to provide a series of particularly attractive excursion sailings from Liverpool to Douglas, every Sunday from 25th June until 20th August. Three hours were allowed ashore and a contract ticket for all nine excursions cost just £1-15s-0d. (£1.75).

A fine study of a pristine-looking **Ben-my-Chree** (4), ready to take up service shortly before the Second World War at Barrow. *(Jeffrey D.Sankey)*

The **Tynwald** (4) being warped out of Douglas inner harbour after her winter lay-up in 1938. *(Stan Basnett collection)*

An outstanding view of the *King Orry* (3) at speed inward bound to the Isle of Man prior to the outbreak of the Second World War. *(Jeffrey D. Sankey collection)*

47

CHAPTER SIX

THE SECOND WORLD WAR 1939-1945

On the outbreak of war on 3rd September 1939 the Isle of Man Steam Packet Company had a fleet of sixteen steamers. The three cargo steamers *Peveril* [2], *Conister* and *Cushag* were retained by the Company and initially the *Rushen Castle* and the *Victoria* were left to maintain the wartime passenger sailings.

The *King Orry*, *Manx Maid* and *Mona's Isle* were converted into armed boarding vessels, and the remaining eight passenger steamers all became personnel carriers and conveyed part of the British Expeditionary Force to France. The old *Tynwald* [3] was moved from Glasgow to the Wallasey Dock, Birkenhead, where she became the accommodation/supply ship HMS *Eastern Isles*.

The principal event of 1940 was Operation Dynamo, the evacuation of troops from Dunkirk, which lasted from 26th May until 4th June. The total number of troops landed in England from Dunkirk is generally accepted as 338,226, and of these 24,669 were brought out on the eight steamers of the Isle of Man Steam Packet Company which took part in the operation.

The 29th May 1940 was perhaps the blackest day in the long and honourable history of the Isle of Man Steam Packet Company. At 05.30 the *Mona's Queen* was approaching Dunkirk and when one mile off the port she detonated a magnetic mine which caused her to break her back and sink. Twenty-four of her crew were lost, seventeen of them from the Isle of Man.

Later that same day the *Fenella* was berthed starboard side to the east mole stone jetty at Dunkirk. She had 650 troops on board when a force of German aircraft bombed the pier at 17.00 with such effect that heavy stone blocks crashed into the side of the ship and her engine room flooded, causing her to settle on an even keel. The Liverpool & North Wales Steamship Company's *St Seiriol* rendered all possible assistance.

The 29th May also claimed the *King Orry* which was bombed in the approaches to Dunkirk and was severely damaged. She was ordered to clear the harbour and the approach channel before she sank. Shortly after 02.00 on the morning of 30th May she sank after her engine room flooded.

The Company had lost three of its steamers in just twenty hours.

The *Mona's Isle* was the first ship to leave Dover when Operation Dynamo started and she brought out 2,634 troops in two round trips. The *Manxman* also made two round trips. On the night of 2nd June, after completing three round trips, the *Ben-my-Chree* was in collision off Folkestone which finished her involvement in the operation. The *Lady of Mann* took 4,262 men back to Dover on four crossings from Dunkirk while the *Tynwald* is recorded as making four round trips and bringing out 8,953 troops.

A fortnight after Dunkirk, Operation Ariel commenced - the evacuation of troops from Le Havre, Cherbourg and Brest. On one sailing from Le Havre the *Lady of Mann* carried as many as 5,000 troops. The *Manx Maid* embarked 3,000 troops at Brest - double her normal complement. The *Manxman* was the final troopship to leave Cherbourg, steaming away to safety as the Germans were entering the port area. Rommel described her as 'the cheeky two-funnelled steamer'. Just before the invasion of the Channel Islands on 1st July 1940, the *Viking* steamed into St Peter Port, Guernsey and took 1,800 children to the safety of Weymouth.

Whilst on passage from Douglas to Liverpool on 20th December 1940, the *Victoria* exploded two mines in her wake but reached port unscathed. When outward bound to Douglas on 27th December and eight miles north-west of the Bar Lightship she detonated another mine which severely disabled her. Fortunately it was flat calm and her 200 passengers were transferred to other vessels. The *Victoria* was towed back to Liverpool. After this incident the Company's passenger operations were transferred to Fleetwood

The *Fenella* (2) and the *Tynwald* (4) were engaged during the early months of 1940 between Southampton and the French ports of Cherbourg and Le Havre. *(Imperial War Museum)*

The *Manx Maid* (1) at Brest on 16th June 1940 during the evacuations from Brittany. Picture taken from the *Lady of Mann* (1). *(Imperial War Museum)*

50

with effect from 28th December 1940.

After her mine damage had been repaired, the *Victoria* did not return to the Company but was requisitioned and fitted out as an LSI (Landing Ship Infantry) before sailing to the Firth of Forth as a target vessel.

In 1941 the *Tynwald* was converted to an auxiliary anti-aircraft cruiser and most of her superstructure was removed. She was commissioned on 1st October and took up convoy escort work in the Western Approaches. The *Mona's Isle* joined the Rosyth Command after refit becoming the A.A. guardship at Methil in the Firth of Forth. From 1941 until the beginning of 1944 the *Ben-my-Chree* was a troop transporter, often sailing as far north as Iceland. In October 1941 the Admiralty requisitioned the *Manxman* and she was commissioned in the Royal Navy as HMS *Caduceus*. She was attached to the Naval RDF (Radio Direction Finding) training establishment HMS *Valkyrie* which had been set up in hotels on Douglas promenade.

HMS *Tynwald* took part in the North Africa campaign and was assigned to Operation Torch. She was at anchor in Bougie Bay, 100 miles to the east of Algiers, when the Italian submarine *Argo* attacked her with two torpedoes in the early hours of 12th

The *Fenella* (2) embarking troops alongside the East Mole at Dunkirk during the evacuation of May 1940. Enemy bombs exploded alongside her, pushing heavy stone blocks through her hull, causing her engine room to flood and the ship to settle. *(Imperial War Museum)*

November 1942. This was the Company's fourth and final war loss.

In January 1944 the *Ben-my-Chree* went to North Shields to be fitted out as an LSI, carrying six landing craft. After this conversion she was in the English Channel, working up for D-Day. On 6th June the 'Ben' was at Omaha Beach as headquarters ship for the 514th Assault Flotilla. Like the 'Ben', the *Lady of Mann* had been converted to an LSI. On D-Day the 'Lady' was headquarters ship for the 512th Assault Flotilla, responsible for landings on Juno Beach near Courseulles. The *Victoria* was present at the D-Day landings at Arromanches, and for some days after landed American forces on Utah Beach.

With the impending end of the war in Europe, the *Viking* was derequisitioned in May 1945 and was overhauled at Barrow. She returned to the Fleetwood service on 18th June, still with her hull grey but with her Steam Packet funnel colours restored. The *Mona's Isle* re-entered passenger service in July 1945, and on the 'Isle's return to peacetime work the *Snaefell* was withdrawn due to her deteriorating condition. The *Manx Maid* was returned to the

Company in March 1945, but was laid up until the 1946 summer season.

The Company's policy of the post-1918 period of buying-in second-hand tonnage was not repeated and when it became reasonable to expect an Allied victory an order was placed with Cammell Laird at Birkenhead for two passenger steamers. With the coming of peace on 8th May 1945 construction was speeded up and the first ship was launched on 22nd November and named *King Orry* [4]. Her design was a development of the 1936 *Fenella* and *Tynwald* and the new ship and her sisters were designed for service throughout the year.

In 1945, prior to the launch of the new *King Orry*, the Steam Packet Company had a fleet of eleven vessels with a total age of 353 years, giving an amazing average age of 32 years. Only four of the fleet had been built to the Company's specifications; the majority of the fleet consisted of second-hand tonnage purchased in the 1920s.

HMS *Tynwald* (4) as an auxiliary anti-aircraft cruiser in 1941. She was sunk by an Italian submarine in November of the following year - the Company's fourth war loss. (*Imperial War Museum*)

CHAPTER SEVEN

POST-WAR YEARS 1946-1961

The *Lady of Mann* returned to Douglas on 9th March 1946 and was given a civic reception. After partial reconditioning by Cammell Laird she re-entered Steam Packet service on 14th June.

Meanwhile, the new *King Orry* [4] ran her trials on 12th April. Captain J.E. Ronan, for many years a Master with the Company and now retired, recalls her first arrival at Douglas: "Probably the most exciting and vivid moment of that time was when the new *King Orry* arrived from Cammell Laird. Along with the other lads from the *Mona's Isle*, I crossed the King Edward Pier to have a look at this new and beautiful ship. We were still in the aftermath of war with its grim austerities, and it was a most wonderful experience to perceive all those modern furnishings and gadgets, the magic of which in later life, when looking over new ships (and there were many), was never quite recaptured."

The *King Orry* [4] was delivered to the Company on 16th April 1946 and she made her maiden voyage from Liverpool to Douglas two days later. The principal service had been transferred back to Liverpool from Fleetwood only ten days earlier, on 8th April.

The *Ben-my-Chree* arrived back at Birkenhead from her war service on 11th May 1946 and Cammell Laird had her ready to enter passenger service on 6th July. The *Manx Maid* was back in service at Whitsun 1946 after being laid up for a year. The *Viking* appeared for the 1946 summer season on 21st June.

A sister to the new *King Orry*, the *Mona's Queen* [4], was launched from Cammell Laird's on 5th February 1946 and she made her maiden voyage on 26th June. On 14th September the *Rushen Castle* (dating from 1898) made her final crossing for the Company. Throughout 1946 the *Victoria* sailed as a unit of the leave service on her original route from Dover to Calais while the *Manxman* was running on the repatriation service from Harwich to the Hook of Holland.

Another new steamer was launched from Cammell Laird on 24th March 1947 as the *Tynwald* [5]. She was very similar to the two earlier post-war new-buildings and entered service on 31st July. The *Victoria* eventually returned to Steam Packet service on 11th June.

The *Mona's Isle* [4] made her final sailings for the Company at the end of the 1947 season and in 1948 she was replaced by the new *Snaefell* [5] which was launched at Birkenhead on 5th March 1948.

The *Manxman*'s contract with the British Government finished in 1949 and she arrived at Barrow on 28th February. The old ship was

The **Lady of Mann** (1) arriving at the Victoria Pier at Douglas. *(John Clarkson collection)*

Top: The ***Mona's Queen*** (4) at her Birkenhead launch on a sunny 5th February 1946. *(Wirral Archives)*

Above: The ***Tynwald*** (5) going down the ways in March 1947. *(Wirral Archives)*

Right: The ***Tynwald*** (5) was the third of the post-war sisters from Cammell Laird at Birkenhead, entering service in July 1947. *(John Clarkson collection)*

surveyed with a view to further service but the costs involved outweighed her life expectancy. The ship was broken up at Preston at the end of 1949.

In 1950 the *Ben-my-Chree*'s appearance was altered by the removal of the cowl from her funnel. The 'Ben' had carried a disproportionately tall funnel from 1927 to the completion of her

war service when it was shortened as it gave her a tendency to roll heavily. After a break of eleven years, services from Douglas to Dublin recommenced in 1950 while the *Manx Maid*'s final passenger sailings took place on 26th August that year. The fifth of the post-war fleet replacements, the *Mona's Isle* [5], was launched from Cammell Laird's Birkenhead yard on 12th October.

The old *Tynwald* [3] of 1891 / *Western Isles* / *Eastern Isles* left Wallasey Dock on 13th May 1951 and was towed to La Spezia for demolition. A few weeks earlier the new *Mona's Isle* made her maiden voyage on 22nd March. A 'personal best' for the Liverpool and Douglas passage was made by the *King Orry* on 23rd May 1951 when she crossed, berth to berth, in 3 hours 18 minutes.

Top. The **Manxman** (2) of 1955 was the last of the Steam Packet's post-war series of six passenger ships and the only one with raised lifeboats. *(John Clarkson collection)*

Bottom: The **Mona's Isle** (5) was the Company's penultimate post-war passenger steamer and was retired in 1980. *(John Clarkson collection)*

A view of Ardrossan showing the **Tynwald** (5) arriving from Douglas. *(Bruce Peter collection)*

The rather spartan atmosphere of the Second Class Restaurant on the **King Orry** (4). *(Wirral Archives)*

The First Class Ladies' Lounge on the **King Orry** (4) *(Wirral Archives)*

The launch of the **Mona's Queen** (4) at Birkenhead on 5th February 1946. She was sold to Greek owners in 1962. *(Wirral Archives)*

For many years the Steam Packet's cargo service from Coburg Dock at Liverpool had been operated by the *Conister* [1] and the *Peveril* [2]. A third vessel was often required and the Company frequently chartered suitable ships. However, a new purpose-built cargo vessel was launched at Troon in August 1951. She was the *Fenella* [3] and was the Company's first motor ship, as well as being the first vessel to be built for the Company in Scotland for 54 years.

The Steam Packet's passenger traffic had always been concentrated into summer peaks, and necessitated the Company keeping a large reserve of vessels for summer-only use. Only two passenger vessels were required during the long winter months and usually six units of the fleet would spend almost nine months of every year laid up at Barrow or Birkenhead.

The principal 'peak' was the weekend of the returning T.T. Week race traffic when the entire fleet would operate a shuttle service around the clock, and the other peaks were the last two Saturdays in July and the first three in August. Saturday 2nd August 1952 was a typical busy day. Leaving Liverpool at 00.27 the *King Orry* had 2,160 passengers on board and on a return sailing from Douglas at 06.15 she carried 1,900. The 'Orry' departed from Liverpool again at 10.50 with her full complement of 2,160 passengers and the day was rounded off with the 16.00 Douglas to Fleetwood sailing with 1,440 passengers: 7,660 passengers carried on one steamer in 24 hours.

Saturday 31st January 1953 produced one of the worst winter storms of the century. As usual, the *King Orry* was on winter service and left Liverpool at 10.55 with 120 passengers. After passing the Rock Light she met NNW force 12 conditions and her log records 'very heavy broken sea, fierce rain and sleet squalls. Vessel pitching and pounding heavily, shipping much water at times.' (It will be recalled that on this stormy day the British Railways car ferry *Princess Victoria* sank on passage between Stranraer and Larne with heavy loss of life). The *King Orry* finally berthed at Douglas at 21.55, exactly eleven hours after leaving Liverpool.

Gales from an easterly point always caused problems at Douglas until the new breakwater was completed in the early 1980s. There was no sheltered berth and at high tide a heavy swell would cause vessels to range up and down the pier. In ESE force 9 conditions on 27th January 1954 the *King Orry* sailed direct from Liverpool to Peel and arrived at the sheltered west coast port after a passage of 5 hours 6 minutes. This was the first instance in post-war years of

The closure of the Fleetwood service in September 1961 saw the *Mona's Queen* placed on the sales list. *(Wirral Archives)*

Peel being used as a diversionary port for Douglas. Peel was regularly used in subsequent winters and during the winter of 1978/79 eighteen diversions were made owing to Douglas being unapproachable in easterly gales.

At the age of 49 years, which had included service in both World Wars, the veteran steamer *Viking* made her final sailings on 14th August 1954. She remained a coal burner to her last day and had been the mainstay of the Fleetwood service throughout her career.

The Isle of Man Steam Packet Company completed its immediate post-war rebuilding programme with the launch of the *Manxman* [2] at Birkenhead on 8th February 1955. She was the sixth and last of the 'King Orry class'. The new ship attracted some criticism in that a] she was not designed as a car ferry, and b] she had not been fitted with Denny-Brown stabilisers.

In 1955 the Steam Packet's fleet consisted of six fine new steamers, plus the pre-war *Lady of Mann*, *Ben-my-Chree* and *Victoria*. The passenger fleet could accommodate in excess of 19,000 passengers at any one time.

At the end of the 1956 summer season the faithful *Victoria* made her final passenger sailings on 17th August and was laid up in the Wallasey Dock at Birkenhead. In January 1957, when the old ship was in her fiftieth year, she was towed to Barrow and the breaker's yard. With the passenger fleet reduced to eight steamers, the Company chartered the Liverpool & North Wales Steamship Company's *St Seiriol* on peak Saturdays in 1957 and 1958.

The *Ben-my-Chree*, thirty years old in 1957, spent the greater part of the 1957/58 winter in No.5 drydock at Cammell Laird's yard undergoing a major refit following her survey. A year later the *Lady*

59

The **Lady of Mann** (1) was certainly the best-loved of all recent Steam Packet vessels and here she is with whistle blasting as she passes one of her consorts on passage to Liverpool. *(E.D.Lace)*

of Mann received similar attention.

The reliability of the turbine steamers was second-to-none. It was almost possible to set a clock by the comings and goings of the Isle of Man steamers as they passed the Rock Light. However, on 3rd December 1958 the *King Orry* was unable to leave Liverpool due to a burst steam pipe in the engine room. This was the only occasion in a thirty-year career that she was unable to sail on schedule because of mechanical trouble.

At the Company's Annual General Meeting on 24th February 1960 it was announced that an order might be placed for a car ferry vessel. "The matter is under careful and earnest consideration," said Mr J.F. Crellin, Chairman of the Directors. In the event an order was placed with Cammell Laird in October 1960.

On Tuesday 1st August 1961 the *Lady of Mann* had to return to Liverpool owing to a bomb scare. Two 'phone calls were received by the Liverpool agents of the Company, Thomas Orford & Son, insisting that there was a bomb on the lower deck, and Captain G.R. Kinley was informed. The 'Lady' was approaching the Bar

Prior to roll on - roll off operations, all the local buses were shipped to the Island by the traditional lift on - lift off method. Here the **Fenella** leaves Douglas. *(Stan Basnett)*

The **Mona's Isle** (5) rolling uncomfortably to starboard as she approaches Douglas in gale-force conditions. It was always the claim of the Steam Packet that they always sailed, whatever the weather! *(E.D.Lace)*

The **Ramsey** was a sturdy little vessel which enjoyed Manx service between 1964 and 1974 when she was sold on. *(Stan Basnett)*

when Captain Kinley decided to return to Liverpool so that the ship could be searched.

The Fleetwood - Douglas service was abandoned at the end of the 1961 summer season as the wooden berth at Fleetwood was in a state of serious disrepair. The *Mona's Queen* sailed on 11th September with flags on her foremast spelling out 'Deeply Regret Fleetwood Goodbye'. A week later the *Mona's Queen* herself was placed on the sales list. The new car ferry building at Cammell Laird, coupled with the closure of Fleetwood, had made her redundant.

The *King Orry* had been winter steamer from 1946 to 1961, apart from the 1950/51 winter. On the morning of 24th December 1961 she was attempting to enter Douglas in a full easterly gale when a severe gust caught her and she fell very heavily on to the south corner of the Victoria Pier, splintering her main belting. She retired to Cammell Laird for repairs, but in 1962 the new car ferry would supersede her as winter steamer, in partnership with the *Manxman*.

CHAPTER EIGHT

THE SIDE-LOADING CAR FERRIES 1962-1977

The Isle of Man Steam Packet Company's first car ferry, the *Manx Maid* [2] was launched from Cammell Laird's yard on 23rd January 1962. The design principle for vehicle loading was simple - a spiral set of ramps at the stern linked with the car deck so that vehicles could be driven on or off at the appropriate level. This overcame the problem of the twenty-foot tidal range at Douglas. At Liverpool the car deck was on the level with the landing stage.

The *Manx Maid*'s maiden voyage was from Liverpool to Douglas on 23rd May 1962. She was the first Steam Packet vessel to be fitted with stabilisers, and although she undoubtedly was a lively seaboat

The official launch party admire the _Manx Maid_ (2) as she slips into the Mersey on 23rd January 1962. (Wirral Archives)

some accounts of rough crossings have been grossly over-sensationalised. In her first season the 'Maid' was used exclusively on the Liverpool - Douglas route.

At the end of 1962 the news broke that the Liverpool & North Wales Steamship Company had gone into voluntary liquidation. The Steam Packet Company stepped in to fill the gap and announced a limited Liverpool - Llandudno service for the summer of 1963. The IOMSPCo actually took over the Llandudno - Douglas route in 1962 following the withdrawal of the *St. Seiriol* in September 1961.

The *Mona's Queen* [4] was sold to the Chandris group in October 1962 and sailed out to Piraeus under the name of *Barrow Queen*. After a complete refit, she sailed in the Mediterranean for almost 19 years as the *Fiesta*.

On 14th February 1964 the *Mona's Isle* was on winter service and had been diverted to Peel due to an easterly gale. The following morning she left Peel breakwater at 06.20 and shortly afterwards her stern ran aground on the rocks behind Peel Castle. Two tugs arrived from Liverpool to tow the 'Isle' to Birkenhead for repairs, and the extensive damage kept her out of service until 14th July, leaving the Company short of one ship during T.T. Week.

A new purpose-built cargo vessel, the *Peveril* [3], arrived at Douglas from her builders at Troon on 7th March 1964, and on the following day sailed on her maiden voyage to Liverpool.

The 44-year-old cargo steamer *Conister* (1) was sold for scrapping in January 1965. To replace her the Ailsa Shipbuilding Company delivered the small cargo vessel *Ramsey*, which arrived at her 'home' port of Ramsey on 28th January.

The final sailing of the *Ben-my-Chree* [4] was from Douglas to Liverpool in the early hours of Monday 13th September 1965. After a leisurely five hour crossing the 'Ben' was laid up in Morpeth Dock, Birkenhead, and the suffix 'II' added, so that the famous name could be given to the Company's second car ferry, building at Cammell Laird's.

The Company's final turbine steamer, the *Ben-my-Chree* (5) ready for launching at Birkenhead on 10th December 1965. *(Wirral Archives)*

Ben-my-Chree (5)

Top: The Second Class Lounge.

Above: One of the vessel's comfortable officer's cabins.

Right: Following her successful launch, the **Ben-my-Chree** (5) was towed to Cammell Laird's fitting-out yard.

(All photos Wirral Archives)

The ***Manx' Maid***'s car deck looking aft with the turn-table in the foreground, it was used for swinging the cars round to face the correct way for disembarkation. (*Wirral Archives*)

The new *Ben-my-Chree* [5] was launched on 10th December 1965. She was the fourteenth (and final) ship to be built for the Steam Packet Company at Birkenhead. She was the Company's last steamer and the last vessel to be built with her passenger accommodation designed for two classes. There was almost an historic meeting on the Mersey that December day for the old 'Ben' should have left Birkenhead for the breakers' yard in Belgium on the same high tide as the new 'Ben' was launched. However, forecast gales delayed the old 'Ben's' departure and it was not until 18th December that she was towed away.

The new *Ben-my-Chree* sailed on her maiden voyage on 10th May 1966. Apart from a few minor differences, she was a repeat of the highly successful *Manx Maid*. On the maiden voyage passengers were invited to inspect the bridge and an excellent 'High Tea' could be taken for 9s.6d. (47.5p).

Four days later the new 'Ben' sailed to Barrow to lay-up for the duration of the 42-day 1966 seamen's strike. The entire Steam Packet fleet was strikebound until 2nd July which resulted in the T.T. motor cycle races being postponed until September of that year.

With effect from 1st January 1967 all the Company's steamers became 'one class' ships for passengers. Considerable savings could be effected by reducing the number of stewards, particularly in the winter months.

Llandudno Pier was not available to the Company in 1967 as the wooden berthing head had fallen into serious disrepair. Whilst not as important as Fleetwood had been, Llandudno nevertheless produced some 30,000 day-trippers every season, and together with the Liverpool to Llandudno sailings provided mid-week employment for the Company's steamers. Two concrete dolphins (mooring posts) were built over the 1967/68 winter and sailings resumed in summer 1968.

The sea link between Douglas and Fleetwood re-opened on Good Friday 4th April 1969 when Norwest Hovercraft placed the 700 passenger, 1,339 ton *Stella Marina* on the route. A daily round trip, increased to two on Saturdays, was planned. The following year the *Stella Marina* was not available and Norwest purchased the elderly *Norwest Laird* (ex David MacBrayne's *Lochiel*) for the service. After thirty years on the Islay route the old ship was worn out; she took six

A powerful view of the **Ben-my-Chree** (5) as she shows a clean pair of heels during speed trials. *(Wirral Archives)*

Glistening in the afternoon light, the **Ben-my-Chree** (5) sits alongside the south Edward Pier. (*E.D.Lace*)

hours on passage and only fourteen round trips were completed during the season.

It was announced in late August 1970 that Ramsey's Queens Pier would be closed to passengers at the end of the season as the wooden berthing head was in very poor condition. In 1906 over 36,000 passengers were embarked or landed at Ramsey Pier but by 1969 this had fallen to just 3,054. The final occasion on which a Steam Packet vessel called at the pier was on 10th September 1970 when the *Manxman* berthed alongside on a Belfast sailing.

Arguably the Steam Packet's most famous steamer, the magnificent *Lady of Mann* of 1930, was nearing the end of her career in 1971. The 'Lady's' final passenger sailing was from Ardrossan to Douglas on the afternoon of Sunday 14th August and she left Douglas for the last time at 17.00 on 17th August on her way to Barrow to lay up, pending sale. In perfect weather the piers and promenades were lined with several thousand people who wished the old ship an emotional farewell as she swept past the harbour entrance to the accompaniment of her triple-chime whistle. The 'Lady' was purchased by Arnott Young of Dalmuir for demolition and she arrived there on the last day of 1971 under tow of the tug *Wrestler*.

The port of Fleetwood re-opened to Manx steamers on 25th

August 1971. A new berth was available and the *Mona's Isle* was rostered to open the new service.

In Summer 1971 there had been an acute shortage of car space and the passenger steamers frequently duplicated the car ferry sailings. The Company's third car ferry, the *Mona's Queen* [5], was named at the Ailsa yard at Troon on 21st December 1971. She became the first passenger motor ship in the Manx fleet and also the first to be fitted with a bow-thrust unit which greatly assisted in speeding up berthing times.

The *Peveril* [3] was converted to a container ship by her builders in early 1972. Her cargo handling cranes were removed and a cellular system for 56 twenty-foot equivalent units (TEUs) was installed. The weekly Ramsey freight sailing was withdrawn and the cargo vessel *Ramsey*, which had made her maiden voyage as recently as February 1965, was effectively redundant as was the *Fenella* of 1951.

The entry into service of the *Mona's Queen* meant that for the first time continuous car ferry working could be maintained during the winter months. Until the 1971-1972 winter, the *Manxman* had been pressed into stints of winter service whilst the *Manx Maid* and *Ben-my-Chree* received their annual overhauls.

As a 'running-mate' for the *Peveril*, the Steam Packet Company chartered the *Spaniel* from the Belfast Steamship Company in 1973 and then bought her outright in November and renamed her *Conister* [2]. The Ailsa Company at Troon converted her to Steam Packet requirements and she was equipped to carry 46 TEUs.

The replacement of the old Liverpool Landing Stage became a priority in 1973. A new and much smaller stage was planned but in the inflationary 1970s the cost of this was spiralling out of control and reached an estimated £1.25 million by the end of 1973.

Over the winter months of 1973/1974, the price of fuel oil quadrupled and the Company was forced to increase the passenger return fare by a massive 36% to £9 with effect from February 1974. The *Mona's Queen* introduced car ferry sailings to Dublin later in the year.

On Bank Holiday Monday 26th August 1974 there were seven Steam Packet passenger vessels berthed together in Douglas Harbour which would never happen again as the *Tynwald* was sold later in the year. It was also announced that there would be no Heysham - Douglas sailings in 1975 as there was 'insufficient passenger potential to meet the additional operating costs.'

The *Manx Maid* struck the Fort Anne Jetty at Douglas whilst

On board the *Manx Maid* when outward bound in the Mersey. *(Wirral Archives)*

69

Top: The **Tynwald** (5) seen here berthed on the north side of the King Edward VIII Pier and about to leave on Monday 2nd August 1971, three blasts on the whistle indicating her intention to all. *(Stan Basnett/Eric Bird)*

Above: The **Manx Maid** (2) carrying the second version of the Company logo which was adopted during 1984. *(Ian Collard)*

Right: The **Ben-my-Chree** (5) arrives at Douglas during some wintery conditions. *(Stan Basnett)*

Seen from the Mersey ferry **Royal Iris**, the **Ben-my-Chree** (5) is seen on 17th April 1980 when making her final approach to the Pier Head. (*John Hendy*)

attempting to berth in bad weather on 13th November 1974, and three weeks later the northern section of the old Landing Stage at Liverpool sank, taking with it the Company's booking office.

The *Manx Maid* was trapped in a Birkenhead dry dock until the end of May 1975. A prolonged industrial dispute had broken out at Cammell Laird which meant finding alternative overhaul arrangements for the rest of the fleet.

However, the 1975 summer season turned out to be very successful for the Steam Packet Company. With fine and sunny weather predominating, the Company carried a total of 909,556 passengers, the highest figure for very many years and a total which has not been exceeded since, nor is ever likely to be. At the end of the summer the *King Orry* made her final crossings on 31st August. She had made 7,412 sailings for the Company in the course of a remarkable thirty-year career, and had steamed 516,770 miles and carried 3,325,500 passengers.

The Company's fourth car ferry, the *Lady of Mann* [2] was

The **Manx Maid** departing on an afternoon sailing from Douglas to Liverpool in July 1982. (*John Hendy*)

The Company's first diesel-powered passenger/ car ferry was the **Mona's Queen** (5) which was built by Ailsa at Troon in 1972. *(Ferry Publications Library)*

The **Mona's Queen** (5) departing from Douglas butting into an easterly to turn, as the strength of wind prohibited turning in the outer harbour. She was the first vessel to be fitted with a bow thruster from new. *(Stan Basnett)*

launched from the Troon yard of the Ailsa Shipbuilding Company on 4th December 1975. For the first time, the car ferries outnumbered the classic passenger steamers in the fleet. The new 'Lady' arrived at Douglas on 29th June 1976, several weeks late. She had missed the T.T. Race traffic which the Company carried with just six vessels. The new ship was a more powerful vessel than her elder sister, the *Mona's Queen*, and did not suffer the teething troubles of the earlier vessel.

Car ferry sailings from Fleetwood were inaugurated in 1976 but the response was less than enthusiastic as only 2,000 cars were conveyed on 88 sailings, an average of just 22 per crossing. Despite the summer of 1976 being the hottest of the twentieth century, the Company reported a drop of 12,000 passengers when compared to 1975.

In mid-January 1977 the Chairman of the Isle of Man Harbour Board announced that roll on - roll off facilities were being considered by his Board, but their provision depended on two major

73

The *Ben-my-Chree* (5) pushes her way out of Douglas harbour in a strong easterly wind. *(Stan Basnett)*

The **Mona's Queen** carefully threads her way through the mudflats of the Wyre estuary ready to berth alongside at Fleetwood. *(Ferry Publications Library)*

factors: 1] the building of a breakwater extension likely to cost around £5 million, and 2] the provision of a linkspan which might require another £2 million. Notwithstanding this statement, the Isle of Man Government later in 1977 agreed to expenditure of £650,000 to support the setting-up of a ro-ro service by a group of Manx businessmen which would operate in direct competition with the Steam Packet Company. This sum would cover approximately half the cost of a linkspan installation in Douglas Harbour.

In 1977 the Company's operating costs were higher than expected; for instance the annual fuel bill amounted to £1,270,000, six times the 1973 figure. With the threat of a new operator commencing on Isle of Man routes in 1978 it was decided to reduce the Steam Packet fleet to six ships and the *Snaefell* was offered for sale. The Steam Packet Directors made an exploratory trip from London to Zeebrugge and back on the Boeing Jetfoil operated by P&O to assess its potential for Manx routes.

CHAPTER NINE

MANX LINE AND THE MERGER

The Manx Line was formed in 1978 by a group of Island businessmen with the intention of providing roll on - roll off services to the Isle of Man. All the Steam Packet Company's car ferries had been specially built to load and unload from existing harbour facilities at Douglas, a system which had limited the size of vehicles carried to cars and light vans. By using Heysham as its U.K. port with its existing loading ramp and a new linkspan at Douglas, Manx Line would overcome this problem.

On 23rd March 1978 the 2,753 ton motor vessel *Monte Castillo* of Bilbao arrived at Douglas and carried out berthing trials. The former Aznar Line vessel then sailed for Leith for a complete refit. Manx Line advertised its new Heysham to Douglas service as

The *Manx Viking* was the former *Monte Castillo* of the Aznar Line and its introduction to the Island was to revolutionise freight handling forever. *(Stan Basnett)*

commencing on 1st June. The new company was accepting bookings up to late May when it suddenly announced that the new service would not be running before 1st July. Owing to industrial strife the *Monte Castillo* (now renamed *Manx Viking*) did not leave Leith until 29th July, arriving in Douglas on 31st July.

The Steam Packet Company had to arrange extra sailings to carry the Manx Line T.T. traffic during the first ten days of June. After further delays the *Manx Viking* made her inaugural crossing from Heysham to Douglas on 26th August 1978. On 8th September, only a fortnight after the service started, one of her diesel engines broke a piston and sailings were again suspended. With the enormous loss of revenue as a result of starting the service so late in the season, plus the high cost of work carried out at Leith and Heysham, Manx Line was rapidly running into serious financial trouble. On 20th October came the announcement that Sealink and James Fisher had taken over the company.

On the night of 1st December 1978, in the first severe easterly gale which had occurred since the installation of the Manx Line Victoria Pier linkspan, it broke adrift and severed its connection with the approach road. Just under two years earlier, in January 1977, the Harbour Board Chairman had said that a prerequisite for siting a linkspan in Douglas Harbour was the construction of an extension to the Battery Pier breakwater to protect the harbour from easterly gales. In its haste to assist the new Manx Line this advice had been ignored by the Government and the result was plain for all to see on the morning of 2nd December.

Without the linkspan facility the *Manx Viking* was unable to operate and was despatched for major overhaul at the Belfast yard of Harland & Wolff on 12th December. There were many on the Isle of Man who considered the Manx Line operation finished.

The run of easterly gales continued throughout the winter of 1978 - 1979 and the Steam Packet Company diverted its vessel to

The **Ben-my-Chree** (5) and the Thoresen ferry **Viking III** at Douglas in Spring 1980. The modern drive-through car ferry was on charter to rival company Manx Line. *(Stan Basnett)*

The **Lady of Mann** (2) approaching Ardrossan. *(Ferry Publications Library)*

The **NF Jaguar** leaves Douglas with a full load of freight for Heysham. *(Stan Basnett)*

Top left: A view from the **Manxman**'s flying bridge during a passage from Llandudno to Douglas in July 1982. *(John Hendy)*

Top right: Looking aft from the same position. Note the ship's gleaming triple-chime whistle. *(John Hendy)*

Excursionists enjoying the ample space provided by the **Manxman**'s boat deck. *(John Hendy)*

The open promenade decks of this class of vessel frequently carried cars when a vehicle ferry wasn't available. *(John Hendy)*

In Autumn 1982, the **Manxman** (2) was purchased by a Preston-based company for use as a night-club. In early October, Captain Peter Corrin took her on a final public sailing from Liverpool to Preston Dock where she is seen on her arrival. *(John Clarkson)*

Peel on eighteen occasions - three times the normal winter average. In November 1979 the Isle of Man Government finally 'grasped the nettle' and approved the expenditure of £7.2 million to protect and extend the Battery Pier at Douglas.

The *Manx Viking* was back on the Heysham - Douglas service in May 1979 using a temporary structure incorporating a Bailey bridge erected on the north side of the King Edward VIII Pier at Douglas. The replacement linkspan finally arrived and was in place on the Victoria Pier in July when the full ro-ro Manx Line service was restored.

Monday 30th June 1980 was the 150th anniversary of the launch of the Isle of Man Steam Packet Company's first vessel, the paddle steamer *Mona's Isle* [1]. Accordingly the *Mona's Isle* [5] was rostered to take a 'Round the Island' excursion to mark the occasion. Due to increased operating costs the Company could no longer keep a reserve of vessels for summer-only use and so the 'Isle' was offered for sale at the end of the season. The Liverpool to Llandudno excursion sailings ceased with her passing.

In September 1980 the Steam Packet Company announced that it had placed a contract for the construction of a linkspan with O.Y. Navire AB of Finland. The linkspan was towed into Douglas on 2nd June 1981 and was ballasted into position on the south Edward

Top: The **Peveril** (4) loading for an evening freight sailing to Heysham *(Richard Kirkman)*

Above: The **Mona's Isle** (6) was the shortest-lived of all Steam Packet vessels. Built as the **Free Enterprise III** for Townsend's Dover - Calais route in 1966, she came to the Island in April 1985 and remained for exactly six months. *(Stan Basnett)*

Right: The **Mona's Isle** (6) arriving at Heysham. *(Ferry Publications Library)*

Following the hasty departure of the ***Mona's Isle*** (6), the Stranraer-Larne car ferry ***Antrim Princess*** was chartered in October 1985 as the ***Tynwald*** (6). She is seen ready to berth at the Victoria Pier during July 1987. *(John Hendy)*

Pier. To operate a new roll on - roll off freight service the Company had chartered the *NF Jaguar* from P&O. The ro-ro service was inaugurated on 19th June and the *Peveril* [3] and the *Conister* [2] were immediately made redundant.

1981 proved to be the Steam Packet's worst year of trading in its long history. After three very good summers, the number of staying visitors to the Isle of Man conveyed by the Company fell by 21.5% and the number of day-excursionists was down by 39%.

The *Manxman* [2] was retained in the fleet for the 1982 season. She was now the very last 'classic' passenger steamer operating in British waters. However, in the generally depressed state of affairs it became clear that it was no longer economically possible to retain her and she was offered for sale at the end of the season, at which time the Llandudno - Douglas sailings would also cease. The *Manxman* was bought for static use at Preston and she sailed from Liverpool under her own steam on 3rd October carrying 1,000

The ***Manx Maid*** and the chartered freight ship ***NF Jaguar*** alongside the Edward Pier during July 1982. *(John Hendy)*

The **Tynwald** departing Douglas for Heysham in July 1987. Her final voyage was in February 1990 after which she was sold to Italian owners. *(John Hendy)*

On board the **Tynwald** (6) in the main bar. *(Ferry Publications Library)*

passengers bound for Preston. At 12.48 she was alongside in the Albert Edward Dock - finally 'Finished with Engines' after 27 years.

The high charter fees for the *NF Jaguar* were a major factor in the Steam Packet's freight service not being viable. Consequently, towards the end of 1982 the Company exercised its option to purchase the vessel. The vessel was painted in Steam Packet colours and renamed *Peveril* [4].

It was becoming evident in 1982 that the Manx tourist industry was in rapid decline. Equally evident was the fact that there was just not room for two passenger ship operators on Isle of Man routes. The Steam Packet Company returned to profitability in 1983 after the two loss-making years of 1981 and 1982. Tenders were received for a new multi-purpose ro-ro vessel, but the lowest price quoted exceeded £20 million.

The *Peveril's* cargo sailings in 1984 were constantly disrupted by strikes and the Company's major freight clients transferred to Sealink/Manx Line. The *Peveril* had the capacity to carry all the cargo requirements of the Isle of Man but in reality was now

By the end of 1978 Sealink had obtained a controlling interest in Manx Line and the **Manx Viking** ultimately carried the Sealink livery. Here the *Manx Viking* is seen swinging in Douglas Harbour. *(Stan Basnett)*

carrying only 50% of that cargo.

The U.K. Government sold Sealink (of which Manx Line was a part) to Sea Containers Limited of Bermuda on 27th July 1984. Thus commenced James Sherwood's involvement in the Manx shipping scene.

At the end of another dismal summer season the steam turbine car ferries *Manx Maid* and *Ben-my-Chree* were offered for sale despite there being considerable useful life left in both of them. A 30% increase in the price of the heavy grade of fuel oil used by the steamers had rendered them totally uneconomic.

On 19th October 1984 the Steam Packet Company purchased the ro-ro vessel *Tamira*, formerly Townsend Thoresen's *Free Enterprise III*. The vessel was lying at Valletta, Malta and Captain Vernon Kinley and a Manx crew flew out to Malta to bring her back to the Clyde. The Company signed an agreement with Burness, Corlett Limited, Naval Architects of Ramsey, in respect of professional advice for refurbishing the ship, which by now was renamed *Mona's Isle* [6].

The Company recorded a loss of £245,244 for 1984, and the year 1985 opened with a veil of secrecy hanging over future operations. No sailing schedules were published and no bookings were accepted for after 31st March. It was obvious that the Steam Packet Company was in severe financial difficulties.

At 09.30 on the morning of 1st February 1985 a press conference was hastily arranged at Imperial Buildings, the Company's head office at Douglas. A joint communiqué was issued from Sealink and the Steam Packet Company outlining a merger of their respective operations, the end of the Liverpool service and the concentration of the main year-round service on Heysham from 1st April. The emotion of Steam Packet shareholders boiled over at a prolonged Extraordinary General Meeting held on 29th March which eventually approved the proposals for the merger.

On the eve of the merger, 31st March 1985, the situation was far from being auspicious. The Steam Packet's new flagship *Mona's Isle* was still at Govan with problems with her fire sprinkler system; the *Peveril* was strikebound at Liverpool; Sealink's *Antrim Princess* was not available to assist, and the *Manx Viking*'s survey certificates were due to expire within 24 hours. The Heysham linkspan was blocked by the striking crew of the *Stena Sailor*.

A basic service was operated by the side-loaders *Mona's Queen* and *Lady of Mann*. More trouble was to follow when the *Mona's Isle* arrived in Douglas on 3rd April only to find that she would not fit either of the two linkspans. A fortnight later the Company announced that the ship had serious deadweight problems and could not carry anything like the loadings expected of her. Due to the extensive new passenger accommodation added, the usable cargo deadweight amounted to just 247 tonnes. Compare this to the 2,220 tons deadweight capacity on the present *Ben-my-Chree*! An inadequate bow-thrust unit meant that the 'Isle' was unmanageable in anything more than a moderate breeze and tugs were required both at Douglas and Heysham to assist in berthing.

The Company had to make arrangements to charter back the *Ben-my-Chree* (5) from her new owners to cover the T.T. period from 25th May until 9th June 1985 and she was re-registered in Liverpool for this period.

The Steam Packet Company Board meeting of 15th August resolved a number of outstanding problems. The *Mona's Isle* would be permanently withdrawn on 5th October after just six months with the Company and would be replaced by Sealink's *Antrim Princess*. The Board would take legal action in respect of the consultancy advice received about the *Mona's Isle*.

The *Antrim Princess* was renamed *Tynwald* [6] and by the end of 1985 her port of registry had been changed from Stranraer to Douglas. Between 1979 and 1985 the holiday seasonal arrivals in the Isle of Man had fallen from 634,616 to 351,240: a decrease of 45%.

In 1986 the Ardrossan sailings were transferred to a weekly seasonal service from Stranraer. A limited Liverpool summer service was introduced on Tuesdays and Saturdays using the *Lady of Mann*. The *Mona's Isle* was sold for £710,502 and was renamed *Al Fahad* for trading in the Red Sea.

The *Manx Viking* was withdrawn from service on 29th September 1986 to be replaced by the *Peveril*. Strike action over manning levels on the *Peveril* led to 58 sailings being lost on four separate occasions, followed by a strike from 4th - 11th December: the longest disruption to services by strikes since 1966.

The **Manx Maid** (2) in the final stages of demolition at Garston in 1986. *(John Clarkson collection)*

CHAPTER TEN

THE TAKE-OVER AND THE SALE 1987-2005

A return to happier Steam Packet days took place in 1987 when the *Mona's Queen* operated a Heysham - Peel - Heysham charter on 4th July. In perfect weather and with 1,600 passengers on board, Captain Jack Ronan sailed the 'Queen' outwards to Peel via Langness and the Calf of Man, and returned to Heysham via the Point of Ayre and Maughold Head.

The crew of the *Tynwald* went on indefinite strike on Tuesday 29th December 1987 over the Company's proposals for revised pay and conditions. The *Tynwald* was at the Heysham linkspan at the outset of the strike and loaded vehicles were trapped on board for 47 days until the industrial action was called off on 13th February 1988.

The *Tynwald* was again off service due to illegal secondary strike action by her crew from 29th April until 14th May 1988. In order to safeguard the T.T. Race Week traffic, the Manx Government

chartered the Skagerrak ferry *Bolette* from Fred. Olsen Lines at a cost of £1 million for three weeks.

At the end of 1988 the Isle of Man Government resolved to dispose of its stockholding in the Steam Packet Company and to compulsorily acquire the two Steam Packet-owned linkspans in Douglas Harbour.

During the early months of 1989 the *Lady of Mann* was given a £2.6 million renovation and an increase in her car capacity at Birkenhead, she returned to service on 26th May with a passenger certificate for just 1,000 (she was licensed to carry 1,600 on her entry into service in 1976).

The *Peveril's* starboard variable pitch propeller mechanism jammed in the reverse position as she was moving astern to the 'Navire' linkspan at Douglas on 14th July 1989. Extensive damage

The **Mona's Queen** was chartered by La Poste in September 1989. She is seen entering Portsmouth Harbour with the **Pride of Le Havre** outward bound from the port. *(John Hendy)*

The *Channel Entente* (ex *Saint Eloi*) undergoing berthing trials at Douglas. *(Richard Danielson)*

The *Saint Eloi* was originally built for the Dover-Dunkirk train ferry service. She is seen here outward bound from Dover to Dunkirk in 1986. *(Miles Cowsill)*

was caused to the linkspan necessitating it being towed to Birkenhead for repairs. Both the *Peveril* and the *Tynwald* had to use the 'MacGregor' linkspan on the Victoria Pier, resulting in much congestion at the height of the summer season.

After being laid up at Birkenhead for over four years the Company's last steamer, the *Ben-my-Chree* of 1966, left for breaking up at Santander on 16th August.

Severe weather at the end of 1989 resulted in all sailings being cancelled on Christmas Eve. For the first time since before the war, daylight crossings were operated on Christmas Day with the *Tynwald* making a return trip to Heysham.

On 7th February 1990 the Steam Packet Company obtained permission from its shareholders to purchase the multi-purpose vessel *Channel Entente* (ex *Saint Eloi*) which had been built in 1972 for the train ferry service from Dover to Dunkirk. Captain Edward Fargher and a Steam Packet crew brought the *Channel Entente* round

Following agreement for the Company to purchase the **Channel Entente**, the vessel operated under this name for her first season prior to her major overhaul and refit in 1990 before becoming the **King Orry** (5). *(Miles Cowsill)*

This view of the **King Orry** (5) clearly shows her new side loading door for operations on the Liverpool service. *(Miles Cowsill)*

The **King Orry** undergoing her major refit in 1990. *(Ferry Publications Library)*

The Cafeteria on the **King Orry** following her refit. *(Ferry Publications Library)*

Drivers' Lounge Area on the **King Orry**. *(Ferry Publications Library)*

Some of the brochures produced by the Isle of Man Steam Packet over the last 32 years. *(Ferry Publications Library)*

Brunnings design agency of Manchester produced some very strong advertising material for the company following the introduction of the *King Orry* and the fastcraft *SeaCat Isle of Man*. *(Ferry Publications Library)*

This outstanding view shows the newly-painted and refurbished *King Orry* (5) outward bound from Douglas to Heysham in 1991. (Ferry Publications Library)

from Dunkirk in early January 1990 and after testing both the linkspans in Douglas Harbour, berthing trials were carried out at all ports used by the Company. After the *Mona's Isle* episode, they were taking no chances!

With the advent of the *Channel Entente*, the *Tynwald* was redundant and she was returned to Sealink after her final Steam Packet sailings on 19th February. The new ship sailed from Douglas to Heysham on her maiden Steam Packet voyage on the afternoon of 19th February, having been delayed for nearly four hours by bad weather. In extremely stormy conditions she immediately proved herself to be a good sea boat, in contrast to the very lively *Tynwald*.

The future ownership of the Company was put in doubt by a takeover bid launched in June 1990 on behalf of Sea Containers, who already owned 41% of the share capital. The bid of £1.15p per share was deemed wholly inadequate and on 2nd August Sea Containers withdrew its bid.

The extra vehicle capacity on the *Channel Entente* and the recently rebuilt *Lady of Mann* made the *Mona's Queen* redundant and she made her final sailing on 3rd September. The *Channel Entente* was given a major refit at Birkenhead in Autumn 1990. After returning to Douglas on 6th December she was renamed *King Orry* [5].

A limited Liverpool and Douglas winter service resumed in

By 1990 Sea Containers became a majority shareholder in the Isle of Man Steam Packet and flush with the success of the **Hoverspeed Great Britain,** a special publicity visit was organised to promote this type of craft as the way to the future for sea travel. *(Stan Basnett)*

The big fleet in at Douglas. The smart looking **King Orry** (5) and the **Lady of Mann** are pictured on the Victoria Pier as **SeaCat Isle of Man** leaves the harbour. *(Ferry Publications Library)*

January 1991 on Saturdays only after a five-year gap and the new service rapidly gained popularity, carrying capacity loads most Saturdays. The Steam Packet Company was recovering from the doldrums of the 1980s, and in 1992 pre-tax profits were up on the previous year to £4.1 million.

Whilst taking the 18.15 sailing from Liverpool to Douglas on 14th November the *King Orry* suffered a steering failure in the Queen's Channel in the Mersey approaches and grounded on Taylor's Bank. Hoylake lifeboat and two tugs went to the scene and the 'Orry' was refloated on the rising tide at 22.30. She was towed back to Liverpool where her 374 passengers were transferred to the Adelphi Hotel. The *Lady of Mann* was immediately brought out of dock and restored the sailings the following day.

In Spring 1993 the Steam Packet Company announced 'with regret' that it had been unable to agree terms with Sea Containers

for the charter of a SeaCat for the summer season.

On 2nd June 1993, at the height of the T.T. race traffic, the *Lady of Mann* was manoeuvring in Douglas harbour on arrival from Liverpool, but instead of going astern into No.4 berth on the Victoria Pier she surged ahead and collided with the Battery Pier. A vast backlog of traffic built up and Caledonian MacBrayne's *Pioneer* operated a Gourock to Douglas sailing while the *SeaCat Scotland* made one return trip to Douglas from Stranraer. The 'Lady' was back in service, with a temporary passenger certificate, on 4th June.

In March 1994 came the surprise news that a SeaCat was to be operated on Manx routes for the summer season and that the *Lady of Mann* would be laid up. At the Company's A.G.M. on 5th May the shareholders expressed their concern and demanded assurances that the Directors were confident of the success of the venture. The events of a decade earlier were uncomfortably fresh in the

The *King Orry* (5) pictured at the Landing Stage, Liverpool with the Liver Building behind her. *(Ferry Publications Library)*

Another busy TT with *King Orry* unloading traffic from Heysham.
(Richard Kirkman)

memories of many shareholders!

The T.T. race traffic in 1994 was carried by the *King Orry*, the *Lady of Mann* and the freight vessel *Peveril*. On 28th June the *Lady of Mann* was laid up at Birkenhead and on that same day the *SeaCat Isle of Man*, on charter from Sea Containers, made her inaugural crossing from Douglas to Fleetwood, taking just 94 minutes for the passage. The following day the SeaCat sailed from Douglas to Liverpool in 2 hours 20 minutes. A £350,000 pontoon and ramp were provided at Liverpool to accommodate the craft.

A long spell of calm and settled weather prevailed in July and August 1994 and it was not until 28th August that gales disrupted the SeaCat schedule. The fast craft was not permitted to sail in waves exceeding 3.5 metres in height. In August 1994 work started on the installation of the Manx Government's own linkspan on the north side of the Edward Pier at Douglas.

During her winter overhaul of 1994/95, the *King Orry* was transferred from the Bahamas register to the Manx register while in

95

The **Lady of Mann** swings in the harbour at the start of another TT season. *(Miles Cowsill)*

May the new Manx Government linkspan arrived from Holland and was lifted into position at the north Edward Pier at Douglas by the floating crane *Mersey Mammoth*.

The problem of how to employ the *Lady of Mann* was solved in the summer of 1995 by chartering her to the Porto Santo Line of Madeira. After operating the T.T. schedules for eighteen days, the 'Lady' was laid up until 17th July when she left Birkenhead on the four-day passage to Funchal, Madeira.

On 11th July the Manx Government finally approved the ten-year 'User Agreement' for its new linkspan. The Agreement required the Steam Packet Company to operate each year a minimum of 486 return passenger services to north-west England / North Wales, of which at least 104 must be to a port in the Liverpool / Holyhead range. At least 63 return services were required to Irish ports. Freight services had to be provided for a minimum of five days per week, with a limited service on the sixth. There had to be a minimum investment in ships, and fare increases had to be pegged to the Manx rate of inflation. In return the Steam Packet Company received sole user rights to the new linkspan.

On 27th September, the *SeaCat Isle of Man* was struck by what was described as a 'freak wave' near the Mersey Bar. The craft sustained some structural damage and the watertight bow visor was twisted. The SeaCat was sent to Cammell Laird for repairs and an official investigation was immediately ordered. The Company warned that, due to her £6,000 a day charter fee, it expected a drop in profits for 1995.

On 30th October 1995 the Steam Packet Directors decided to dispense with the fast craft in 1996. The *Lady of Mann* returned from her Madeira charter in November and the *Mona's Queen* was sold to new owners in the Philippines. The 1995 results showed pre-tax profits down by £4 million to just £458,000. Half of this was due to the high cost of operating the SeaCat.

On 29th March 1996 it was announced that the Isle of Man Steam Packet Company had lost its independence after 166 years of operation and that Sea Containers Isle of Man now owned 58% of the shares. Subsequently most remaining shareholders accepted Sea Containers' offer and by the date of the 166th and final Annual General Meeting of the Members of the Company on 2nd May, Sea Containers controlled over 95% of the shares and the

Dressed overall at Fleetwood, the *Lady of Mann* (2) makes an impressive sight prior to a special sailing to Douglas. *(Ferry Publications Library/Captain Vernon Kinley)*

In 1994 and 1995 the *Claymore* provided weekend voyages to Douglas, Isle of Man. She is seen here arriving from Scotland in her second season. *(Miles Cowsill)*

The **Ben-my-Chree** (6) manoeuvres slowly up the New Waterway in Rotterdam prior to undertaking sea trials. *(Ferry Publications Library)*

The **Ben-my-Chree** (6) in her final stages of fitting out at Van der Giessen-de Noord. *(Ferry Publications Library)*

The bridge is lifted onto main structure of the **Ben-my-Chree** (6). *(Ferry Publications Library)*

The **Ben-my-Chree** (6) leaves Douglas on her morning schedule to Heysham during her first couple weeks in service with the company. *(Miles Cowsill)*

The **SeaCat Danmark** covered the fast ferry operations of the company in 1998. *(Miles Cowsill)*

Company was delisted on the Stock Exchange. With no fast craft in operation in 1996, it was left to the *King Orry* and the *Lady of Mann* to provide the passenger services.

In early 1997 it was announced that an order had been placed with Van der Giessen-de Noord of Rotterdam for a new ro-pax vessel to replace the *King Orry* and the *Peveril*. At 125 metres in length the new vessel would be built to the near maximum dimensions for using the harbours at Heysham and Douglas.

The *SeaCat Isle of Man* returned to Manx waters on 21st May 1997. Her programme of sailings was far more intensive than in 1994 and 1995. Following the T.T. traffic sailings, the *Lady of Mann* opened a new Liverpool - Dublin service on 12th June, providing a scheduled six-and-a-half hour passage. Given favourable tides, the 'Lady' often completed the passage in well under six hours.

The keel of the new ro-pax vessel, to be named *Ben-my-Chree* [6], was laid on 28th October 1997. At this early stage concerns began to be voiced about her limited passenger certificate for just 500 passengers.

100   An early morning scene at Douglas Harbour. The **Lady of Mann** (2) is pictured on the Victoria Pier with the **SeaCat Isle of Man** loading for her morning sailing to Liverpool. Meanwhile the **Ben-my-Chree** (6) is discharging following her 06.15 arrival from Heysham. *(Ferry Publications Library)*

The *SeaCat Isle of Man* was replaced by *SeaCat Danmark* for the 1998 summer season and she entered service on 21st May. During the 1998 T.T. race period, the *Lady of Mann* operated her usual busy schedule and on 17th June she sailed for the Azores on a three-month bareboat charter, sailing between eight ports within the group of islands.

The Liverpool - Dublin service, operated by the 'Lady' in 1997, was taken over by the monohull fast craft *SuperSeaCat Two* in 1998. The new craft, restricted to sailing in seas of under three metres in height, had a very mixed summer and suffered from recurrent technical problems as well as bad weather cancellations. The *Lady of Mann*, back from her charter to the Azores, covered as many of the cancelled services as was possible.

The new £24 million Steam Packet ro-pax vessel *Ben-my-Chree* arrived in Douglas from her builders on 6th July 1998. She entered

service in 'freight mode' when the ro-ro freight vessel *Peveril* was withdrawn from service and laid up at Birkenhead.

The 'Ben' entered full passenger service on 4th August 1998 and to enable the new vessel to settle in, the Steam Packet kept the *King Orry* in service as back-up vessel until 29th September, after which she was laid up at Birkenhead. The 'Orry' was quickly sold for £2 million to Fion s.p.a. of Italy and left the Mersey for the last time on 23rd October carrying the name *Moby Love*, registered in Naples, but still in full Steam Packet livery.

In October 1998 the Manx Parliament appointed a Select Committee on the Isle of Man Steam Packet Company with a remit to look at the frequency and quality of passenger services following criticism of the new *Ben-my-Chree*. A couple of months later the Company announced that the 'Ben' would not in future carry more than 350 passengers per sailing, which was considered a 'comfort level'.

The **King Orry** (5) leaving Douglas in her final Steam Packet livery. *(Miles Cowsill)*

The *SuperSeaCat Two* leaves Douglas on her early morning sailing to Liverpool. *(Miles Cowsill)*

For the summer seasonal fast craft services, the *SeaCat Isle of Man* returned to Manx waters, commencing her sailings on 31st March 1999. The *Lady of Mann* returned to Douglas on 26th May with 900 passengers on a day excursion from Llandudno, and the next day brought in 600 trippers from Fleetwood. These early season day cruises have been a popular feature of the 'Lady's' programme since they were introduced in 1997.

Following the T.T. period, the *Lady of Mann* retired to dock until 23rd July. Rather than go on charter to the sunnier climes of the Azores, the 'Lady' was retained as back-up for the *Ben-my-Chree* during the peak summer season until 12th September. The late autumn and early winter of 1999 saw prolonged periods of stormy weather which led to very active spells of service for the *Lady of Mann* to cover fast craft cancellations during December when she served the Liverpool - Dublin and Liverpool - Douglas routes.

The Steam Packet's 2000 summer season got into full swing with the T.T. motor cycle traffic at the end of May and six vessels were used: the *Ben-my-Chree*, the *Lady of Mann*, the *SuperSeaCat Two* and

A late evening scene at Douglas as the *SuperSeaCat Three* arrives from Liverpool. At times the Italian-built craft found hard to maintain her schedules especially during bad weather. *(Miles Cowsill)*

THE TAKE-OVER AND THE SALE 1987-2005

The *Lady of Mann* (2) at Cammell Laird shipyard in Birkenhead showing the external alterations which were undertaken to comply with the latest SOLAS requirements. *(Ferry Publications Library)*

'Three' and the *SeaCat Isle of Man* and 'Scotland'. Following the T.T. traffic the *Lady of Mann* sailed to the Azores for another three months on charter.

Following two difficult winters, the *Lady of Mann* was scheduled to provide the Liverpool - Douglas winter service from early November 2000 until the end of February 2001.

The 25-year-old *Lady of Mann* entered Cammell Laird's Birkenhead yard at the end of February 2001 for work to start on her refit and SOLAS upgrading. The most visible feature is the new high-speed rescue craft fitted to her starboard side boat deck.

The year 2001 was dominated in the United Kingdom by the outbreak of foot and mouth disease. The Manx Government took the decision to cancel the annual T.T. motor cycle races as part of the precautions to try and prevent the disease reaching the Isle of Man. The Steam Packet normally carries over 35,000 passengers, 15,000 motorcycles and 3,500 other vehicles in connection with the races. The *Lady of Mann*'s Irish Sea schedule was cancelled completely, but she was away to the Azores yet again on her annual three-month charter to Acor Line.

In early 2002 the Steam Packet Company agreed a five-year extension to the 'User Agreement' with the Manx Government concerning the linkspan on the north Edward Pier at Douglas.

Following the cancellation of the T.T. races in 2001, there had been some uncertainty as to how well the event would be supported in 2002. However, the final outcome, according to Manx Tourism Minister David Cretney, was "the highest recorded figure for T.T. ferry traffic for at least 20 years". The intensive schedules worked during the T.T. period allow little flexibility if things go wrong, and the *Ben-my-Chree* had to be withdrawn for emergency repairs on 28th / 29th May during which time the *Lady of Mann* provided extra sailings.

On 24th March 2003, Sea Containers announced that it had put the Isle of Man Steam Packet Company up for sale with a price tag of £150 million. The Manx Government immediately indicated that it was not interested in buying or putting money into the Company.

During its association with the Isle of Man, dating back to the 1985 merger with Manx Line, Sea Containers introduced the ro-

The evening sun captures the **Ben-my-Chree** (6) coming astern at the King Edward Pier inward bound from Heysham. The Dutch-built ship has proved to be extremely reliable and is the main lifeline of the Company's year-round operations. *(Miles Cowsill)*

pax vessel *Ben-my-Chree* and successfully weathered the storm of protest caused by her passenger accommodation. Sea Containers also pioneered the use of large fast craft in Manx waters.

The new owners of the Isle of Man Steam Packet Company were Montagu Private Equity who purchased the Company from Sea Containers for £142 million. The deal was effective from 30th June 2003. Hamish Ross, the Steam Packet's Managing Director, commented: "We are delighted that Montagu have chosen to acquire the Steam Packet under its existing management team." Once again the Company was now very much its own master.

It was announced in December 2003 that additional passenger areas were to be built on the *Ben-my-Chree* at a cost of £1.5 million. The new accommodation allows the vessel to carry her full passenger complement of 500.

The *Ben-my-Chree* returned to service in early February 2004 following the extension to her accommodation aft which provided a new Quiet Lounge and bar. The existing reclining seating lounge forward was converted to make a new 1st Lounge to bring the

During 2006 the 81m **SeaCat Diamant** was on charter from Hoverspeed during the TT period. She seen here leaving the Victoria Pier berth for Liverpool sailing on 3rd June. *(Stan Basnett)*

This interesting view during the TT period of 2004 shows the **Ben-my-Chree** (6) and **Lady of Mann** (2) loading for their evening sailings to Heysham with the **Rapide** having just arrived from Belfast. *(Miles Cowsill)*

The **SeaCat Isle of Man** operated her last season on the Irish Sea for the Steam Packet Company in 2004. She is seen here swinging off the berth outward bound to Liverpool. *(Miles Cowsill)*

vessel in tandem with the facilities offered by other ships in the Company's operations. During the major refit of the *Ben-my-Chree*, the *Lady of Mann* covered for her absence with the Swedish-owned ship *Hoburgen*.

The Isle of Man had a record T.T. season for 2004 and once again a variety of vessels supported the operations during the period, including the *SuperSeaCat Two* and the *Rapide*. Once again, the *Lady of Mann* went south to the Azores on her charter and returned again to Irish Sea operations in late October. During the winter period there were no fast craft operations, leaving only the conventional vessels to maintain services to the Island. In spite of a very severe winter, the Company were able to maintain operations at most times. The *SeaCat Isle of Man* was put up for sale at the end of the season and was acquired during early 2005 by a new operator between Liverpool and Dublin, following the decision of the Isle of Man Steam Packet Company to withdraw from this route.

CHAPTER ELEVEN

LADY OF MANN - HER LAST FIFTEEN YEARS

The Steam Packet was experiencing considerable operational problems with the *Tynwald*, the mainstay of the year-round service, In the late 1980s, with the *Lady of Mann* and the *Mona's Queen* providing additional summer season support. There were emerging plans to find a replacement vessel for the *Tynwald* (eventually leading to the acquisition of the *King Orry*), but the two traditional side-loader ships still offered the flexibility of operation to ports without linkspans. However, declining traffic indicated that only one seasonal vessel could be justified in service in the future. Neither of the side-loaders

offered the quality of on-board facilities that were becoming the norm in the wider ferry industry, and the *Lady of Mann*, the faster and younger of the two vessels, was selected for wholesale refurbishment.

The mix of business on Isle of Man services was also changing, with growing volumes of car traffic and a reduced dependence on the traditional day excursion foot passenger. The 1976-built *Lady of Mann* had been constructed with capacity for 1,600 passengers, but this was reduced to 1,200 in early 1988 to meet changes in safety regulations after the *Herald of Free Enterprise*

The **Lady of Mann** (2) makes a magnificent sight when inward bound on a 'light' sailing to Douglas from Heysham in June 2004. *(Miles Cowsill)*

The Promenade Cafe was fitted out in light colours with comfortable banquette seating helping to create a bright, welcoming atmosphere, *(Ferry Publications Library)*

accident. She could carry 100 cars in her original configuration, but if the fleet was to be rationalised this capability would have to be increased to meet the modern mix of traffic demand.

The project to rebuild passenger facilities on the *Lady of Mann* was announced in October 1988. In a sign of the company's determination to raise quality standards, the London-based Portland Design Associates were selected to produce a radical reconfiguration of the passenger areas, and they applied significant creativity to the design contract to produce a transformation of the passenger experience. The plan also envisaged increasing the vessel's car carrying capacity by 30 vehicles through the creation of an upper car deck accessed from the internal spiral ramp. The contract for the refit was awarded to Wright & Beyer of Birkenhead, and the total cost of the project was £2.6 million.

The rebuilding of the *Lady of Mann* was the largest project ever undertaken at the shipyard. The conversion work began in Birkenhead on 16th January 1989, and the vessel was quickly grit-blasted and painted in red-lead, with her original passenger accommodation removed and the former passenger doors on the shelter deck replaced with sheet metal.

On 'A' deck, the original metal decks were timber-clad to create a more traditional look, and new cabin accommodation was provided. The former Promenade deck – 'B' deck – became the main passenger deck, with seating lounges, the ship's information bureau, the galley and the Promenade Café, as well as the shop and passenger toilets. In a reflection of the new style, furniture was outfitted in pastel colours, with blue, green and pink shades predominating. 'C' deck hosted the 'Triskale' bar and further passenger lounge accommodation and a baggage room, and there was capacity for 30 cars in the newly created upper garage area. The main car deck was 'D' deck and beneath this on 'E' deck could be found the new duty-free shop for Irish services, the cinema and the family room, the only part of the original accommodation that did not receive an upgrade at this refit.

The *Lady of Mann* retained the traditional company colours of

Tasteful use of pictures added to the modern feel of the makeover in the Promenade Cafe. *(Ferry Publications Library)*

Rich carpeting in lounge areas combined with burgundy seat coverings to give a feeling of opulence. *(Ferry Publications Library)*

Portland Design set new standards in interior decor for the company, and later brought homogeneity to the fleet with their work on the *King Orry*. The Cafe Express lounge is typical of their work. *(Ferry Publications Library)*

The *Lady of Mann* (2) leaving the port of Velas on São Jorge Island, whilst on charter in the Azores. *(Bryan Kennedy)*

The *Lady of Mann* (2) at Whitehaven on one of a number of pre-season day trips operated by the Company. *(Bryan Kennedy)*

The *Lady of Mann* (2) swings in the inner harbour of Douglas with the backdrop of the Central Promenade behind. *(Miles Cowsill)*

The 'Lady' was sold for further service to Greek operators SAOS Ferries and extensively altered at the stern to allow the carriage of commercial vehicles on their routes between the Greek Islands. *(Ferry Publications Library)*

Another view of the former **Lady of Mann** (2) under going re-building work at Perama shipyard. *(Ferry Publications Library)*

a plain black hull, white superstructure and red funnel topped in black. A large and distinctive company roundel was added to her forward superstructure beneath the wheelhouse, with a double rope motif wrapping around the vessel and the words 'Isle of Man Steam Packet Company' tastefully applied at the forward end on each side.

The refit brought the *Lady of Mann's* gross tonnage up to 3,176 tons from 2,990 tons. Her new configuration increased her car carrying capacity by 30% to 130 cars and vans. She still retained her side loading capability and the spiral ramps that allowed her to load in port at all states of the tide.

The original plan envisaged the *Lady of Mann* returning to the Isle of Man in readiness for a recommissioning ceremony on Friday 19th May, with opportunities to show off her new style with two trips from Douglas to Peel, followed by promotional sailings to Londonderry, Belfast and Dublin, but delays to the work forced the cancellation of these events. In the event, her first departure was the 19:00 from Liverpool to Douglas on 26th May, a week later than planned, with work to her 'A' deck cabins still not complete. The *Lady of Mann* was officially recommissioned by Mrs Norman Corlett, the wife of the company chairman, in a ceremony in Douglas Harbour on Sunday 28th May. The vessel then undertook an evening cruise to the Calf of Man, taking in circuits around Port St Mary and Port Erin bays, before returning north up the coast to Laxey and back to Douglas.

With the refurbishment works still incomplete but the busy TT period looming, the *Lady of Mann* operated with a reduced certificate for 950 passengers and 50 crew until she could return to the Wright & Beyer shipyard for completion of the works on 15th June. Finally in a finished state, she returned to service with her new 1,000-passenger capacity, by taking the 09:15 Douglas-Dublin departure on 7th July. She proved a very successful vessel in her new guise, and became the company's sole seasonal passenger vessel when the *Mona's Queen* was withdrawn from service in 1990.

For the next fifteen years she proved to be a versatile ship for the compant covering the TT, winter refits and charter work for the company. In September 2005 it was announced that the *Lady of Mann* had been sold to SAOS Lines of Greece. She left the Mersey for the last time on 22nd October. She was transformed into a stern-loading ferry and remained in service in Greece for the next six years until she was scrapped in Turkey in 2011.

Renamed the **Panagia Soumela** she is seen here on the (right) at the port of Agios Kirikos on the island of Ikariai in April 2008. The view above shows the extensive work to the stern for car access and additional passenger accommodation. *(Bryan Kennedy/Ferry Publications Library)*

CHAPTER TWELVE

NATIONALISATION: IN SAFE HANDS

The Company had hoped to replace the monohulled *SuperSeaCat Two* for the 2005 season but nothing suitable could be sourced. Unfortunately, she suffered some damage while leaving dry dock in March that year after which she had to return to dry dock for a short time. The vessel was crewed from the Island for the season but the project to replace her with a new fast craft was put on hold following the decision of the Isle of Man Government to subsidise air fares to promote tourism. This resulted in a 12% reduction in sea passengers.

As the 2005 season got underway it was generally felt, although not officially announced, that it would be the final season of operation of the last of the conventional Steam Packet ships, the *Lady of Mann,* and a number of special excursions were operated in the few days before the TT Festival. This included a two-day 175-mile sail to Troon where she was built and day trips to Barrow, Fleetwood and Llandudno. Immediately after TT, the *Lady of Mann* went off to the Azores for a three-month charter and so was not in Manx waters for the actual 175th anniversary celebrations.

In previous years a Sea Containers vessel from the Belfast – Troon service had been chartered during TT but as that service had closed, the fast craft *P&O Express* was brought in to provide some night sailings from and to Larne. The *Sea Express 1* (ex *SeaCat Isle of Man*) was chartered back and the *River Lune* operated additional freight services to Heysham.

The 175th anniversary Round the Island excursion on the *Ben-my-Chree* was considered to be the climax of the celebrations, Captain Roger Moore sailing the 'Ben' close in at his home village of Port St Mary, followed by a pass of the Chasms and of the rounding the Calf of Man before she sailed right into Port Erin Bay and turned inside the remains of the breakwater. The

'Ben' was by far the largest vessel to ever achieve this.

During September 2005 it was announced that the *Lady of Mann* had been sold to SAOS Lines of Greece for services in the northern Aegean Sea. She left the Mersey for the last time on 22nd October, her passing representing the true end of an era. The *SuperSeacat Two* completed the seasonal sailings to and from Liverpool but continued with the Friday to Monday sailings through November and December although her use during the winter caused some concerns due to the bad weather operating restrictions imposed on her.

In late 2005 the Company was purchased by Macquarie Bank based in Sydney, Australia although by early 2006 there were no apparent changes in the manner in which matters were being run.

Overall passenger figures for 2005 showed a 6% drop with Liverpool down by 7% while Dublin and Belfast/Larne were down by 36% and 31% respectively. Figures improved during the first couple of months of 2006 with passenger numbers up by 4.5% but shortly after these figures had been announced, the Isle of Man airport reduced landing fees for aircraft to enable airlines to reduce fares. Given that a new vessel was required, this move was not going to encourage the new owners to look favorably at investing in the Steam Packet.

When the 2006 timetables were published in February, the whole TT period was omitted and it appeared that the *Lady of Mann* had been sold before any thoughts on replacing her had been agreed! The *SuperSeaCat Two* returned after a refit at Birkenhead in March 2006, initially covering for the *Ben-my-Chree,* that was away in dry dock.

Six vessels were used during the 2006 TT Festival but with the centenary TT in 2007 there were concerns about the

The *SuperSeaCat Two* prepares for her afternoon sailing to Liverpool, while the explorer vessel *Fram* can be seen at Douglas whilst cruising the Irish Sea and Scotland. *(Miles Cowsill)*

availability of vessels to accommodate the large numbers expected. While the effect of the Macquarie take over had not been seen in any operational sense, the Headquarters building, Imperial Buildings, was sold to the Isle of Man Government for £8m. There were growing concerns over the future of services and the proposals for a new fast craft seemed ever distant.

The *Ben-my-Chree* operated what was billed as its annual Round the Island trip in July 2006 in superb weather conditions. Meanwhile a memorial plaque to commemorate those Steam Packet staff who had lost their lives in the two World Wars was unveiled at the National Arboretum in Staffordshire in August 2006.

The *SuperSeaCat Two* suffered a main gearbox failure on 22nd July, a situation that required the removal of the box and subsequent reduced speed sailings for some time. This period was extended until 9th September before the former *SeaCat Isle of Man* was re-introduced on 11th September. The re-certification of the *Sea Express 1* (ex *SeaCat Isle of Man*) meant that it would be available to assist during TT 2007. The *Ben-my-Chree* ran aground in the Heysham Channel shortly after

The *Ben-my-Chree* arrives at Douglas on her afternoon sailing from Heysham with the *Lady of Mann* on the Victoria Pier pending an evening TT sailing to Liverpool. *(Ferry Publications Library)*

The **Emeraude France** was chartered during 2007 in place of the **Sea Express 1** following her accident in the Mersey. *(Miles Cowsill)*

departing from Heysham with the overnight sailing on 3rd November but fortunately there was no damage caused. Captain Peter Corrin retired as Marine Operations Manager after 38 years with the Company.

Work to replace the usual Isle of Man berth linkspan at Heysham got underway during early 2007. A much needed upgrade of the passenger facilities at Heysham was also undertaken with the work scheduled to be completed by February 2007. That year's timetable confirmed that both the *SuperSeaCat Two* and *Sea Express 1* (ex *SeaCat Isle of Man*) would operate alongside the *Ben-my-Chree* thereby allowing civilised timings for the sailings to Dublin and Belfast.

The *Sea Express 1* collided with Greek bulk carrier *Alaska Rainbow* on the Birkenhead side of the Mersey in thick fog on 3rd February 2007 and was holed below the waterline. Fortunately, no injuries to any passengers or crew were suffered on either vessel. The *SuperSeaCat Two* was in dry dock and so arrangements were made for the *Ben-my-Chree* to sail to the

The **Sea Express 1** collided with Greek bulk carrier **Alaska Rainbow** in the Mersey in thick fog on 3rd February 2007 and was holed below the waterline. She is seen here at the Landing Stage after the accident. *(Ferry Publications Library)*

The *Viking* swings in Douglas Harbour following her late morning sailing from Liverpool. The *Snaefell* is pictured on the Victoria Pier pending her sailing to Dublin. *(Miles Cowsill)*

Top: Incat hull No.026 appeared back on the Island resplendent in the new, and by far the best, livery in 2008. She was renamed **Snaefell** (6). *(Miles Cowsill)*

Above: The **Ben-my-Chree** sporting the new company livery which was in introduced in 2008. *(Miles Cowsill)*

Right: A fine view of the **Stena Caledonia** leaving Douglas for Heysham during her charter in 2007. *(Miles Cowsill)*

Twelve Quays terminal at Birkenhead on Saturdays and Sundays between 3rd and 18th March. These were the first ever sailings by the Company between the Isle of Man and Birkenhead and the 'Ben's' first visit to the Mersey in passenger service. The collision meant that the *Sea Express 1* would not be available for the TT sailings. The report into the collision showed that the Greek vessel was not mentioned in the traffic report given to the *Sea Express 1* as it entered the Mersey as it was expected that the *Alaska Rainbow* would be out of the way by the time the fast craft had arrived at the Pier Head. Following agreement with the insurers, the *Sea Express 1* was repaired, renamed *Snaefell* and repainted, with the work due for completion around the end of January 2008.

With the *Sea Express 1* out of service, a sister craft, the 74 metre *Emeraude France*, was chartered and was made available throughout the 2007 TT period. Delays in getting the TT schedule confirmed resulted in an apology to all passengers who had paid their deposits for TT travel, suggesting that some changes in their travel arrangements might be required. The centenary TT provided a challenging time for the Company and the 5,000 or so bookings that had to be changed at short notice. In the event some 94,000 passengers were carried over a three-week period along with 46,000 vehicles. Most sailings were operated by the *Ben-my-Chree*, *SuperSeaCat Two*, *Emeraude France* and *P&O Express*. The traditional ferry *Stena Caledonia* (ex *St David*) was chartered for two weekends, her first visit being on 2nd June.

Hamish Ross retired from the position of Managing Director at the end of June, having been in the position since 1996 when the Company was purchased by Sea Containers. He was replaced by Mark Woodward.

After the TT Festival, the Company returned to its normal summer schedule only to face the appointment of a Tynwald select committee to look into its fares and whether these were compliant with the user agreement. The Manx Grand Prix of 2007 attracted an additional 25% of bikes on the back of the TT.

Following the success of the *Ben-my-Chree*'s sailings to Twelve Quays earlier in the year, it was decided to provide a winter weekend service to the Mersey port from November through to February. These sailings received a mixed reaction, primarily because in recent winters it had been possible to sail to either Heysham or Liverpool at weekends but now only Birkenhead. It was hoped that the 'Ben' could use the Pier Head in future winters.

As part of a re-branding, the *SuperSeaCat Two* was renamed *Viking*, both she and the *Snaefell* appearing with gloss black hulls, a bright red boot topping, a darker red funnel with wider black bands and the website address in white capital letters on the black hull

Seaside Shipping Ltd a recently formed Isle of Man Company had lodged a petition of doleance in the high court challenging the user agreement and the use of the linkspans.

After around five years of searching for a new fastcraft, it was finally announced on 19th May 2008 that the Company had purchased the 96 metre *Incat 050* to replace the *Viking* (ex *SuperSeaCat Two*). Purchased in Tasmania, the vessel left Hobart on 23rd June arriving in Portsmouth in mid-July for an extensive refit by Burgess Marine and Fleet Support Ltd. Passenger accommodation was increased from its existing 400 to over 800. New accommodation modules were added to the vessel which was capable of conveying lorries and coaches when operating on the Heysham route. The total project cost, including purchase of the vessel, was quoted to be in the region of £20m. Built in 1998, the vessel had operated in Australia and New Zealand before being chartered to the US Military in 2001. This meant that she had very low operating hours compared to other vessels of similar age.

The rebuilt *Snaefell* finally returned to service on 12th May, just in time for the TT period that saw passenger levels back to those of the 2006 festival. The North Channel's *Stena Caledonia* returned for two weekends at TT as did the *P&O Express* from Larne.

Improvements and maintenance at Liverpool Pier Head led to diversions to Heysham but when the *Viking* returned there, it was found that vessel did not fit the temporary ramp provided, resulting if further diversions. More work was completed over the following winter to accommodate the new Incat craft for the 2009 season.

Fishing debris in the approach to Douglas Harbour damaged two of the water jets on the *Viking* on 26th July and one of the propellers on the 'Ben' the following day. A few days later the

The **Ben my Chree** (6) has given excellent service and reliability since her introduction and has proved herself as an excellent all weather vessel and has sailed in all but the worst weather conditions. *(Stan Basnett)*

The **Manannan** passes the cruiseship **Regent** off Douglas Head en route to Liverpool. *(Miles Cowsill)*

Viking was damaged when a squall forced her back against the landing stage at Liverpool just as she was departing.

Juan Kelly retired as Chairman in June 2008 and was replaced by Robert Quayle, while Hamish Ross stood down as a non-executive Director. The legal challenge by Seaside Shipping Ltd to the user agreement was blocked by the Isle of Man Courts although the court made no ruling regarding the user agreement restricting trade under European Legislation.

A public competition resulted in the name *Manannan* being chosen for the *Incat 050* which was expected in Manx waters during early April 2009. Some delays had been encountered with the rebuild following a particularly cold winter but all main structural work had been completed by the end of February. Following completion by Burgess Marine, the *Manannan* sailed to Douglas arriving on 11th May. On her approach she rendezvoused with the *Snaefell* as she was on her way to Liverpool, before circling round the *Ben-my-Chree* departing for Heysham. Her maiden voyage for the Company was to

121

Another afternoon sailing to Liverpool for the *Manannan* as she leaves Douglas in June 2019. *(Miles Cowsill)*

Liverpool on 22nd May.

Following TT 2009, the *Viking* was offered for sale or charter and went off to Atlanticoline for service in the Azores at which time a side door was fitted. In September it was confirmed that she had been sold to Hellenic Lines and re-named *Hellenic Wind*. Although the *Snaefell* had begun the season and continued to operate alongside the new *Manannan*, her future was also in doubt.

Seaside Shipping successfully appealed against the decision of the courts to dismiss their application challenging the access to the Douglas linkspans.

The *Manannan* suffered her first in service failure on 3rd September having to return to Douglas but she was back in service later the same day. Her last day of operation for the 2009 season was a day later than planned due to bad weather. Overall, the vessel was well received although the one issue commonly raised was the passenger lift which had at times been a little temperamental.

A group of local hauliers began a container service between Glasson and Ramsey in November 2009, thus reducing the freight levels conveyed by the Steam Packet, while just short of 600,000 passengers were conveyed during 2009. The operation later moved to Douglas to overcome tidal issues associated with Ramsey and continued to use the Norwegian *Ingeborg Pilot* which had taken one of the larger freight contracts from the Steam Packet. The service eventually ceased in February 2011 after insufficient growth had made its continuation unsustainable.

The Icelandic volcanic ash cloud of April and May 2010 brought severe disruption to air traffic serving the Island but had the opposite effect on Steam Packet passenger numbers, with over 9,000 passengers carried, an increase of 50% on normal loadings for the time of year.

Immediately following the successful 2010 TT Festival, one of the *Manannan*'s main Caterpillar engines suffered a serious crankshaft issue. The approaching school holidays led to the decision to operate at reduced speed rather than withdraw the vessel from service and not to be left out, the *Snaefell* suffered a similar failure a short time later necessitating her running at reduced speed. The *Snaefell* was offered for sale in late 2010 but remained available for service until the spring of 2011 after which her summer duties were covered by the *Manannan*. The

Following the serious damage caused to *Manannan*'s trim tabs on 1st April 2015, P&O *Express* was drafted in to operate a sailing from Larne. Unlike the many TT sailings, this trip was during daylight hours and is seen here entering Douglas harbour. *(Barry Edwards)*

The P&O *Express* edges back towards the King Edward Pier berth at Douglas while the *Manannan* occupies the Victoria Pier on 8th April 2015. *(Barry Edwards)*

extra capacity provided by *Manannan* enabled the Company to launch day trip packages to retail centres in the North West along with attractions such as Chester Zoo, flower shows and theme parks.

The Company announced a new ownership structure in April 2011 with a refinancing deal struck with a group of banks led by Banco Espírito Santo, based in Portugal. The share capital of the Company previously owned by a group of Australian pension funds and Macquarie, was transferred to Sealion Isle of Man Ltd, a company owned by the Steam Packet Company's banks.

The *Snaefell* called in at Douglas on 30th June 2011 on her way to a two-month charter to the Port of Piraeus (Athens). It was later confirmed that she had been sold to Taxyploa Maritime Company, re-named *Master Jet* and registered in Cyprus. Her sale reduced the Steam Packet fleet to just two vessels.

In early 2012, the silting of Heysham became a major talking point, a problem that remains today, and led the Steam Packet to suggest that it was considering a move back to Liverpool to avoid such problems. Heysham Port were restricting under keel clearance in the approach channel, with potential effects on sailing times.

During the evacuation of Dunkirk on 29th May 1940, the *Mona's Queen* (4) had been one of three Steam Packet vessels to be lost. To mark the seventieth anniversary of the event, her anchor was retrieved from the sea bed off the French coast and, after restoration at Cammell Laird, was returned to the Island on 31st October 2012 and placed at a new memorial at Callow Point in Port St Mary. The memorial was unveiled on 3rd June, the *Manannan* providing a salute after having diverted to pass by during a sailing from Liverpool to Douglas. On the same day, a restored lifeboat from the *Lady of Mann* (1) took part in the Queen's Jubilee Pageant on the Thames, flying the Company flag for the event.

The start of the 2013 fastcraft season was disrupted by weather as were the *Ben-my-Chree's* sailings at the same time. The 'Ben' collided with one of the mooring dolphins at Douglas while berthing on a wild evening on 1st May. Repairs were completed to the vessel by the following evening, while the berth took around a week to repair.

No sooner had the challenge by Seaside Shipping Ltd been resolved with an out of court agreement, than a new threat loomed with the formation of Ellan Vannin Line, a new company planning to operate freight services from late 2013 and passenger sailings in time for TT 2014. In response to a public meeting called by Captain Kurt Bochholz of Ellan Vannin Line, the Steam Packet Chairman Robert Quayle issued a statement stating that history had proven that there was insufficient traffic to support two operators and that the recent financial restructuring had halved the Company debt, thus enabling the Company to consider future developments and new vessels with confidence.

The *Manannan* completed its 2013 season having achieved a 100% technical reliability and 98% service reliability.

Winter weather played its part in disrupting the *Ben-my-Chree's* services to Heysham and Birkenhead, one storm damaging one of the stabiliser fins, requiring the vessel to go to dry dock to

have it removed for repair. Once removed, it was discovered that the fin was more severely damaged than first thought and in the event it was May before the fin was replaced. The Company announced that the freight vessel *Arrow* had been chartered to cover for anticipated use during TT and to cover for the *Ben-my-Chree* while she was in dry dock.

The Ellan Vannin Line saga persisted, with the company having a number of meetings with the Island Port Authorities and threatening to take the matter of use of the linkspan to the EU if a positive answer was not forthcoming. The Chief Minister and Department of Infrastructure issued a statement outlining the user agreement in place between Government and the Steam Packet for the use of the linkspan, and their rights to allow the occasional visiting vessels to use the facility.

TT figures for 2014 showed a 7.5% increase over those of 2007, with 12,050 motorcycles and 36,800 passengers conveyed. The *P&O Express* operated its usual charters from Larne and the *Arrow* was used to assist with Heysham freight requirements. An electrical fault at Liverpool on 25th August resulted in the return sailing to Douglas being cancelled after it had been fully loaded. Sadly, in their frustration some passengers caused some damage onboard the vessel and in the Liverpool departure lounge, the incident requiring Merseyside police to be called.

Just as the Company was gearing up for the Festival of Motorcycling, news came that all shares in Banco Espírito Santo had been suspended by the Bank of Portugal. The bank soon announced a restructure to deal with its debts and the Steam Packet made a statement stating that it was aware of the issues but did not anticipate any impact on its operations.

As 2014 ended, negotiations regarding a new user agreement had been ongoing for three and a half years without consensus. The agreement was due to expire in 2020 with an option of an extension for six years. The replacement of the *Ben-my-Chree* was already on the agenda but without an operating agreement, there was little chance of persuading shareholders to invest in a new vessel.

The Liverpool landing stage was also approaching the end of its useful life and was the subject of discussions between Peel Ports, the Steam Packet and Isle of Man Government. The Isle of Man Government was keen to secure long term access to the landing stage and at about the same time also requested

On Tuesday 4th September 2018, The **Ben-my-Chree** sets off from Douglas with the daily 08.45 sailing to Heysham, passing mv **Arrow** anchored in Douglas Bay. The **Arrow** had been in Manx waters providing additional freight capacity during the Festival of Motorcycling that had finished the previous weekend. *(Barry Edwards)*

expressions of interest from operators who might be interested in supplying sea services to the Island. It was suggested that eight operators had expressed interest which put any plans for a new Steam Packet vessel in jeopardy, as a user agreement was essential to make it viable to finance such a purchase.

The *Manannan* suffered serious damage to her trim tabs during a sailing from Douglas to Dublin on 1st April 2015, the vessel coming to a stop off Port Soderick, while attempts were made to rectify the issue. Debris had been ingested and the vessel had to be taken out of service, not returning until 11th April. The *P&O Express* and the freighter *Arrow* were drafted in

to cover sailings and provide freight back up. Bad weather and further technical problems occurred through April and May, the suitability of the Company to provide the lifeline services to the Island being questioned in Tynwald. Silting at Heysham and bad weather continued through into June and the TT Festival and towards the end of 2015, P&O announced that it was not retaining the *P&O Express* which meant that the vessel would not be available for additional sailings for the TT period in 2016.

On 23rd March 2016, shortly after the start of the fastcraft season, the *Manannan* collided with the Victoria Pier while approaching with the evening sailing from Liverpool. A few

The **Ben-my-Chree** makes an annual trip round the Isle of Man, usually in mid-June. The sailing provides an opportunity for passengers to see the Manx coastline from just a few hundred yards out to sea. On 22nd June 2019, the vessel is seen turning just below Milners Tower on Bradda Head at the entrance to Port Erin Bay. *(Barry Edwards)*

passengers were injured and needed hospital treatment. The *Arrow* was summoned from the Channel Islands to assist, while the *P&O Express* covered one sailing from Larne. Meanwhile the *Manannan* went to dry dock and returned to service on 3rd April. The *Arrow* remained in Manx waters to cover for the *Ben-my-Chree's* biennial dry dock but the problems continued with the ship suffering with propeller vibration necessitating a return to dry dock followed by a fuel pump issue a few days later.

The *Ben-my-Chree* sailed to Holyhead for berthing trials on 21st May, following an announcement by the Company that it was considering using the port as a back-up. Nothing appears to have come of this plan but the *Manannan* made a similar trip to Holyhead on 30th June. The *Manannan* also visited Larne for trials in March 2017 with the *Ben-my-Chree* following in July.

On 24th May 2016 a Steam Packet press release outlined plans for a £170m investment in two new vessels, port facilities and fare promotions. This was a bold attempt to show its intention to retain its Isle of Man business. Eventually on 18th July, Tynwald was asked to note the terms of the offer from the Company and instruct the Department of Infrastructure to continue negotiations with the Company, while considering all other options for achieving a solution that would benefit the

127

On 31st May 2020 *Manannan* suffered a technical problem shortly after departing with the 10.00 sailing to Heysham. The vessel limped back to Douglas and is seen here entering the harbour with the *Ben-my-Chree* unusually berthed on the outside of Victoria Pier. Final berthing assistance was provided by diesel tug *Wendy Ann*, built in 1934. *(Barry Edwards)*

Island. The Steam Packet offer was withdrawn making the future of services beyond 2026 unclear.

On the evening of 12th February 2017, the *Ben-my-Chree* hit the headlines when after being caught by a particularly strong gust of wind, she collided with the King Edward Pier. Both the ship and the quay were damaged but, the vessel returned to service the following evening.

In spite of the lack of the *P&O Express*, the Steam Packet carried 14,037 motorcycles and 36,500 passengers during the 2017 TT Festival. Commenting on the figures, the Company said it was awaiting a response to its offer of two new vessels and associated improvements to be able to increase its future capacity at this vital time of year.

Rumours began to circulate that after 178 years of service, the Isle of Man Government was considering nationalising the Steam Packet Company, despite the medium-term investment required. This was followed by an announcement in local media that Tynwald had approved harbour improvements to the tune of £80m, to include a cruise berth on the outside of Victoria Pier (£11m) and improvements to King Edward Pier (£14.8m) but that the Steam Packet had not been consulted. The improvements to King Edward Pier included the ability to berth a 'Heysham Max' vessel of up to 142m long. There would also be a new linkspan on Victoria Pier, capable of handling any vessel. Meanwhile, in the Mersey, the costs of replacing the Liverpool landing stage had moved to above £30m and so the Isle of Man Government was looking to buy a site at the Princes Half Tide Dock in order to have its own terminal in the city.

On 23rd May 2018 the Isle of Man Government announced that it had concluded a deal to purchase the Steam Packet for £48.3m with an agreement to provide an additional £76m as a loan to the Company. The value of the two vessels by 2026 was estimated at just £4.4m. The value of the deal to the Government assumed investment of £85m in new or almost new vessels by 2023 while the existing management was retained.

Plans to move the Steam Packet berth at Liverpool, 800 metres from the Pier Head to the Princes Half Tide Dock continued with planning permission sought for the development. The first images of the proposed new terminal building were released on 29th October 2018 and were put on public display

129

in Liverpool but, interestingly not on the Island. In mid-November work started to install underground facilities for the new road that will link the terminal to the road network. The project is expected to cost the Manx taxpayer £30m and the formal planning application for the actual building was made on 11th December.

In a statement on 26th September 2018 the Isle of Man Treasury Minister provided some information on the details surrounding the Government ownership of the Steam Packet. It stated that it would not be involved in the day to day operation of the Company but promised that the service offered and the Company would be fit for purpose, while acknowledging that this would be complex.

A detailed document outlining the relationship between the Isle of Man Government and the Steam Packet was put before Tynwald in the third week of November 2018. It confirmed that the Company would be operated at arm's length from Government and that the shareholder agreement would come into force on 1st January 2019. The document outlined some basic requirements of the board, including the convening of extraordinary general meetings on a twice-yearly basis. There should be at least five directors with a minimum of three non-executive directors, one of whom will be the chairperson. Members of Tynwald are not permitted to be directors. The Government will be entitled to invite advisers and political members of the Treasury and other third-party members as observers. The Company will have to seek approval from Government if it wishes to enter into an agreement or contract worth in excess of £2.5m, or if it wishes to enter into a mortgage for a ship.

Following the purchase of the Steam Packet, the Government launched a public consultation about the services. There were 4,862 responses representing about 6% of the total population of the Island. Questions included preferred destinations, whether conventional ferries or fast craft should be used and whether ticket prices were considered fair. The results of the survey showed that 2,970 (61.1%) wanted the fast craft service to continue while 1,617 (33.3%) said they preferred the year-round conventional ferry. Of those that used these sailings, 25.6% travelling to Dublin and 26.9% to Belfast were dissatisfied with the frequency of the service then offered. Additionally, the

opportunity was also taken to introduce a new Sea Services Agreement with the Company replacing the old User Agreement. Perhaps the most notable part of the agreement was the replacement of the *Ben-my-Chree* with a new vessel by the end of 2021. The *Ben-my-Chree* is 125.2 metres long with the longest capacity at Douglas being 136 metres while Heysham and the new Liverpool Ferry Terminal are both 142 metres. Approval has now been granted to extend the capacity at Douglas to 142 metres, allowing the replacement for the *Ben-my-Chree* to be up to 17 metres longer if desired.

Following approval in Tynwald, the new Sea Services Agreement was signed in a low-key ceremony on Monday 3rd June 2019, by Minister for Infrastructure Ray Harmer MHK, and Chairman of the Isle of Man Steam Packet Company, Robert Quayle. Tynwald approved the refinancing of the Company debt on 24th October 2019, supporting the recommendation from the Treasury Minister for the Company to borrow the £76m from an outside source.

The Steam Packet launched an on-line survey in November to gauge views on future investment in a new vessel. Questions related only to the replacement of the *Ben-my-Chree* and sought views on items such as seating, catering, lounges, wifi coverage and charges.

Lars Ugland was appointed as a non-executive director of the Steam Packet Company and became Chairman at the beginning of April 2020, following the retirement of Robert Quayle on 31st March. Mr Ugland had been a member of the Isle of Man Shipping Association since 2007, serving additionally as Honorary Norwegian Consul between 2011 and 2019.

A ceremony was held at the site of the new Liverpool Terminal building on Friday 17th January 2020, attended by the Chief Minister Howard Quayle and Infrastructure Minister Ray Harmer. The £38m project is due for completion in July 2021 with the Government also announcing that plans were being drawn up to refurbish the facilities at Heysham over the next two or three years.

As the new decade began, life around the world was about to change, possibly forever, as the Covid-19 pandemic took hold. In response to the threat posed by the virus, the Isle of Man required anybody arriving on the Island after 17th March, to

Two artist impressions of the new ro-pax due to enter service with Steam Packet in 2023. *(Isle of Man Steam Packet Company)*

self-isolate for 14 days while on Friday 27th March, the borders were closed completely.

Initially, the *Ben-my-Chree* continued her twice daily trips to Heysham for freight. From 15th April the *Manannan* took over the daytime sailings to and from Heysham while the *Arrow* was called in to make the overnight trips to the Lancashire port until 29th April. This allowed the *Ben-my-Chree's* crews to have a full 14-day break and self-isolate in line with Government guidelines. The *Ben-my-Chree* returned to operate the overnight sailings from 30th April, while the *Manannan* covered the daytime sailings.

The *Ben-my-Chree* has been with the Company for just over 22 years and during that time her two main engines have accumulated over 225,000 running hours. She has operated over 33,250 sailings and covered a distance of 1.86 million miles. With a new vessel on the horizon, expected in service around the beginning of 2023, the *Ben-my-Chree* will then become the spare ship, providing charter income to the Company when not required in Manx waters and allowing an increase in sailings at peak times, as well as covering for dry dock periods for both the new vessel and the *Manannan*. It is anticipated that *Manannan* will be replaced by around 2026.

New Vessel due in 2023

After several months of anticipation, the Steam Packet Company announced on Friday 31st July 2020 that it had signed a contract with Hyundai Mipo Dockyard, Ulsan, South Korea for a new purpose built ro-pax vessel.

The new ship will be slightly bigger than the Ben-my-Chree and have considerably more passenger space as well as increased lane meterage for vehicles. It will also be more environmentally efficient and achieve better maneuverability in poor weather conditions.

Final design work is not expected to be completed until around mid-2021, when construction will start. The new vessel is expected in Manx waters towards the end of 2022, with an entry into service in the spring of 2023.

The procurement process began during the autumn of 2019 with an invitation for builders interested in the bespoke vessel to tender, resulting in several expressions of interest from across the globe.

It remains to be seen if a second identical ship is ordered to replace the *Manannan* later in the decade.

CHAPTER THIRTEEN

LONG LIVE THE KING

When the erstwhile *King Orry* raised the Italian flag and sailed down the River Mersey for the final time under her new name of *Moby Love* of 23 October 1998, few could have imagined that the longest part of her career was still ahead of her. Yet, for the relative bargain price of £2 million, Moby Lines had secured a fine vessel that would give them another 19 years' service, longer than she spent with either Sealink or the Steam Packet Company. When she finally left their fleet in 2017, this sturdy ferry would find a fourth owner, willing to invest in a major refit, to see her hopefully continue sailing for many more years to come. Sadly, matters have been much more tumultuous in her fourth incarnation than in the stable careers she previously enjoyed.

Mediterranean-Bound

When the *King Orry*'s Manx service ended, she was 23 years old and one of the last of her generation still to be sailing around the UK. Indeed, her two multi-purpose design-cousins, the *Vortigern* and *Chartres*, had long since headed for the warmer climes, as had the related *Hengist*, *Horsa* and *Senlac*. All were equally to have the longest parts of their careers in the Mediterranean, but it is again the former "King" that looks set to outlive her peers in commercial European service.

Moby Lines, formed in Italy in 1959 as Navigazione Arcipelago Maddalenino (Nav.Ar.Ma), had undergone dramatic expansion in the 1980s, with their fleet boosted by several former Northern European ferries. The business was, perhaps surprisingly, able to survive the tragic *Moby Prince* fire in 1991, following her collision with a stationary oil tanker off the coast from Livorno. Despite this crisis, by the mid-1990s the Company had been able to rejuvenate itself, and was once again in growth, based on a family-friendly identity and vibrant, eye-catching hull artwork which they had pioneered, long before it became popular elsewhere. The second route that the company had

inaugurated, in 1966, was from Piombino, on Italy's West Coast, to Portoferraio on the popular holiday island of Elba. The company subsequently used Piombino as a base to launch their first longer service, to Bastia, Corsica the following year. Fast forward 30 years, and Moby had purchased the former *King Orry* to bolster their Elba fleet as well as reinstating summer-only crossings on the Piombino to Bastia route which, since it's debut in 1967, had long since been usurped by the (slightly shorter) crossing from Livorno.

Italian Refurbishment

Unlike many Mediterranean operators, by the 1990s, Moby Lines took the approach of thoroughly refitting the interiors of their second-hand acquisitions. The core layout of the vessel remained unchanged, with most saloons also initially retaining their previous purpose - the major exception being the aft video lounge and shopping centre on C Deck, which was gutted and converted into a larger shopping and video-games area, arranged around a spacious central lobby. Two of the smaller saloons on B Deck were also repurposed; the King's Head snug being equipped with short rows of cinema-style seating to become a private conference room and the small passenger lounge amidships becoming an executive lounge, with seats arranged around a boardroom table.

Yet, although the purpose and layout elsewhere remained as previously, the once-homely accommodation of the *King Orry* was refurbished (almost) throughout the Moby's distinctive corporate style, emerging with a dark blue colour scheme, across the majority of furniture and flooring, along with mirrored ceiling panels. The former Coffee Lounge forward on C Deck was also remodelled, with a much larger central bar servery installed, whilst a new bar counter was added in the forward part of the cafeteria on B Deck. Away from the public areas, signage from her Manx career did remain - not least in the former King's

A classic view of the **Moby Love** swinging off the port of Piombino. (*Richard Seville*)

Head, where the bar itself was unaltered, complete with Steam Packet Company logos. The most significant change to the vessel, however, was the installation of a new bow visor, converting her to a drive-through vessel. As designed, the potential for such a conversion had always been built-in, and indeed the plans drawn up in the mid-1980s to lengthen and/or stretch her for Sealink showed a visor being installed - but it was only to become a reality when she left the UK shores. During this major refit, she also gained the suffix 2 to her new name, reflecting the fact she was the second *Moby Love*, after the former Belgian Sealink RMT ship *Prins Philippe* of 1973, which had been sold in 1993, in the wake of downsizing after the *Moby Prince* disaster.

Two Decades at Elba

As the *Moby Love 2*, she re-entered service at Piombino in April 1999, displaying her own unique Moby hull art designed by the cartoonist Mordillo, featuring two of his trademark characters in - befitting her name - humorous romantic scenes. Although initially intended to sail on the 4.5 hour crossing to Bastia, as well as the hour-long shuttle to Portoferraio, in reality, her service to Corsica was brief and she was soon dedicated to the Elba route. With heavy demand across a lengthy summer season, Moby would offer at least hourly (if not more frequent) departures on this link, in competition with (the then) States-run Toremar. Here she ran alongside a fleet of ferries once known in the UK, including Sealink's *Earl Godwin* as the *Moby Baby*, the

133

The ***Moby Love*** arriving at Piombino still very much showing her orginal lines from her days in British waters. *(Richard Seville)*

Teistin of Strandfaraskip Landsins as *Moby Ale* and Sally Line's *The Viking* as the *Moby Lally*. At off-peak times, this fleet would be reduced to just 1-2, with the others laid up or refitting. As one of the larger units, the *Moby Love* (the 2 was dropped from her name in 2002) could often be found in Genoa during the winter, just a short distance from where she was built.

During her long association with Elba, the *Moby Love*'s available passenger accommodation was gradually reduced. With no need for passenger cabins, both the original cabins beneath the vehicle deck and those in the new block added by the Steam Packet Company on A Deck eventually became derelict. Meanwhile, the saloons on B Deck were increasingly closed off

to the public, with the cafeteria closed and catering limited to a snack service in the main forward lounge on C Deck. Until the end of her Italian service, reminders of her previous career did remaining, if you knew where to look. The filled-in train tracks were still visible on her vehicle deck, the original bell inscribed with both the names *Saint Eloi* and *King Orry* remain on her foredeck, and her builders plate was still in situ outside the Verandah Bar, always proudly polished.

In 2015-2016, the ever-astute Moby Lines announced the purchase of two further ferries to join their fleet - the long-inactive *Galaxy*, from European Seaways, and the *European Voyager*, from European Ferries. Both were relatively elderly, and

The **Moby Love** presents her bow to the quay, no need for linkspans in this part of the Mediterranean. *(Richard Seville)*

The **Moby Love** arrives off the port of Piombino. *(Richard Seville)*

tired, vessels - perhaps surprising acquisitions at first sight. The key, however, lay in the scarcity of ferries of their modest size, with Moby being able to buy them relatively cheaply and then invest in comprehensive refurbishments. The *Galaxy* was bought first, in late 2015, becoming the *Moby Kiss*, and was deployed in 2016 on a Livorno to Bastia to Nice link. The *European Voyager* was acquired in late 2016, for the Elba fleet, being renamed as the *Moby Niki*. However, after just one year serving Bastia, the *Moby Kiss* was also transferred to the Elba station, meaning that in 2017 two new ferries came to this route. It was evident that their arrival would spell the end for some of the older ferries, but

the withdrawal of the *Moby Love* alongside the older *Moby Baby* was a little surprising. However, with Moby having also previously purchased their one-time rival Toremar, the *Moby Love*'s capacity was not needed, whereas the smaller vessels, such as the *Moby Ale*, gave the fleet additional flexibility.

To Greece

The two withdrawn ships were laid up in Genoa and offered for sale as a pair. Despite rumours of a sale as early as February 2017, it was not until October that year that the former *King Orry* was moved to Greece. The two ferries were purchased by Portucalence Shipping, an established Greek business, apparently

Left and right: Two views on board the **Moby Love** showing the former forward coffee lounge of the **King Orry**. (Richard Seville)

with the intent for refitting them for the commercial service. The *Moby Love* was renamed the *Aeolos*, while the *Moby Baby* became the *Anemos*. Whilst the latter was to languish before ultimately been scrapped, refurbishment work started almost immediately on the *Aeolos*. The work initially took place in Greece, before she was towed to Turkey, apparently for the removal of asbestos, being moved back in August 2018. Work gradually continued across 2018. Structurally, her after sundeck on B Deck was extended, the derelict block of cabins on A Deck was removed, and permanent sun shelters were built above her bridge wings. Internally, it was evident that a comprehensive modernisation was underway.

Initial mockups suggested that she would be deployed under the auspices of Hellenic Med Ferries, likely within the Greek island trades where her now (relatively) compact size made her an ideal prospect for secondary routes, and where so many of her former Sealink fleet-mates had enjoyed lengthy careers. No details of her proposed employment were confirmed, however, and instead, it was announced that for the 2019 season, she would be chartered to Atlanticoline for summer service in the Azores (just as the *Lady of Mann* had been previously). Alas, it was not to be, for despite been rechristened as the *Azores Express*, and

even with the Atlanticoline name painted on her hull, the charter was abruptly cancelled just before it was due to start, the reason cited being that she was not ready. By this stage, her renaissance was almost complete; with her appearance further altered by the installation of larger, full height picture windows in her forward superstructure on B Deck. Internally, her accommodation has been transformed. Throughout, she features brand-new fittings, with contemporary muted greys and beige the dominant colours, enlivened by brighter yellow and red in parts -and wood-effect laminate flooring throughout. Major changes to the layout include on C Deck, where the previous shopping and videogames area has been swept away and replaced by a new reception lounge; while amidships the side lounges had been opened up with the removal of the luggage storage areas, and a new business-class, recliner lounge added to starboard. On B Deck, a luxurious new VIP lounge has been created amidships. The quality and style place her amongst the highest standard vessels in the Mediterranean.

Chaos & Uncertainty

Apparently left scrambling to recoup their investment, when almost all summer deployments would have been locked, her

The former forward cafeteria of the *King Orry* looking very different from her days with the Steam Packet. *(Richard Seville)*

The verandah bar on the *King Orry* was a popular venue for bikers during the TT Races. *(Richard Seville)*

owners did succeed in finding a short-term emergency charter for her during August. In the north-east Aegean, the island of Samothraki had suddenly been left almost entirely isolated, when both the vessels of local operator SAOS Ferries broke down at the height of the summer peak. The Greek authorities arranged for the *Azores Express* to be dispatched to take up the route between Alexandroupolis on the mainland and the island harbour of Kamariotissa. However, despite loading for, and departing on, her first sailing, as she approached her destination, she reportedly experienced mechanical problems. Facing a maiden arrival at a port with very narrow confines, her Captain took the decision to return to the mainland without docking. Although it was initially promised she would return as is possible, ultimately she returned to Piraeus without making any further attempts to sail.

Today, she lies waiting for new employment at Perama, a challenge undoubtedly made far harder by the coronavirus pandemic with the devastating impact on ferry traffic in the Greek islands and elsewhere. Given the huge investment that has been made in her refurbishment, and her excellent condition as a result, it seems likely that the owners will hold out to find gainful commercial service for her. It is very much hoped that they will succeed.

Awaiting her fate, the *Moby Love* laid up in Genoa September 2017. *(Richard Seville)*

Looking down on the former ***Moby Love*** at one of drydocks at Piraeus harbour, whilst the vessel undergoes a major refit, including the addition of fixed sun shelters to bridge wings. *(Captain Apostolos Kaknis)*

This view shows the removal of the additional cabin block aft of her funnel and also the new extended area over the stern on her boat deck. *(Captain Apostolos Kaknis)*

Looking very different from her days in British and Italian waters, the **Azores Express** is pictured in the final stages of her conversion at Perama. *(Dimitris Mentakis)*

Part of the upper car deck on the **Azores Express**. *(Spyros Roussos)*

This view shows the extended accommodation over the stern to provide additional outside deck area for passengers and a covered area for the crew. *(Spyros Roussos)*

The new reception lounge on C Deck on the **Azores Express.** (*Spyros Roussos*)

Amidships side lounge. (*Spyros Roussos*)

Part of the new cafeteria on the **Azores Express** following her major overhaul in Greece. (*Spyros Roussos*)

The former coffee lounge forward on C deck on the *Azores Express*. *(Spyros Roussos)*

The former cafeteria on B Deck showing new full height windows. *(Spyros Roussos)*

The former verandah bar on the *King Orry* still remains a bar area on the *Azores Express* leading out to the stern passenger area. *(Spyros Roussos)*

The new VIP lounge amidships on B Deck on the *Azores Express*. *(Spyros Roussos)*

No gangways in Greece; the *Azores Express* now provides an escalator from the car deck to her main passenger accommodation. *(Spyros Roussos)*

The new outside deck area at the stern on the *Azores Express*. *(Spyros Roussos)*

ACKNOWLEDGEMENTS

The **King Orry** unloads during a busy TT season with pleasure steamer **Waverley** on a rare visit to Douglas. *(Richard Kirkman)*

The authors would like to thank Mark Woodward for writing the Foreword to this new edition on the history of one of the world's most famous shipping companies, which celebrated its 190th Annivsary during 2020.

Thanks go also to Richard Kirkman, Richard Seville and Barry Edwards for their valuable input to the book.

The publishers are also greatful to following for photographic material: Stan Basnett, E.D Lace, John Clarkson, Bryan Kennedy, Bruce Peter, Antonios Kioukas, Spyros Roussos and Richard Danielson.